Qur'an for
Astronomy and Earth
Exploration from Space

By the same author

— *Islamic Environmental Systems Engineering: A Systems Study of Environmental Engineering, and the Law, Politics, Education, Economics, and Sociology of Science and Culture of Islam*
(Also in Malay and Indonesian translation)

— *Teaching Islamic Sciences and Engineering: International Comparisons, and Case Studies from King Abdul Aziz University*
(Also in Malay)

— *Islamic Science and Public Policies: Lessons from History of Science.*
(Also translated into Malay, Urdu, and Arabic)

— *Quran for Astronomy and Earth Exploration from Space.*
(Also in Arabic)

— *Islamic Thought in the Rise and Supremacy of Islamic Technological Culture: Water Resources and Energy.*
(Also in Arabic)

— *Water Resources Sciences and Engineering in the Quran: Indexes, and Explanation of Selected Passages*
(Also in Arabic)

— *Economics in the Quran: Indexes, and An Introduction*
(Forthcoming, English-Arabic, and Arabic editions)

Qur'an for Astronomy and Earth Exploration from Space

S. Waqar Ahmed Husaini

Goodword
B·O·O·K·S

© S. Waqar Ahmed Husaini, Third edition, 1999
Second edition, 1996, First edition, 1994
Reprinted, 2002

Published by
Institute of Islamic Sciences,
Technology and Development (IISTD)
1512 South Stelling Road,
Cupertino, CA 95014 U.S.A.
Web site: http://www.islamicscience.org

Major Distributors:
The Islamic Foundation, Markfield Center, Ratby Lane,
Markfield, Leicester LE67 9SY, U.K.
Tel: 44-(0)1530-244944. Fax: 44-(0)1530-244946
Web site: www.islamic-foundation.com
E-mail: publications@islamic-foundation.com

Islamic Book Service (American Trust Publications)
2622 E. Main Street, Plainfield, IN 46168 U.S.A.
Tel: 317-839-8150. Fax: 317-839-2511

Sound Vision
1327 W. Washington Blvd., Chicago, IL 60607, U.S.A.
Tel:1-800-432-4262. 312-226-0205. Fax: 312-226-7537
Web site: www.soundvision.com
E-Mail: info@soundvision.com

ICNA Book Service (Islamic Circle of N. America)
166-26 89th Ave., Jamaica, NY 11432 U.S.A.
Tel:1-800-903-0099. 718-657-4090. Fax: 718-658-5069
Web site: www.icna.org   E-mail: islambooks@aol.com

H.A.D.I. (Human Assistance & Development International, dba IslamiCity)
P.O. Box 4598, Culver City, CA 90231-4598 U.S.A.
Tel: 310-937-9845. Fax: 310-937-9846
Web sites: shop.IslamiCity.com & www.islam.org/iistd
E-Mail: hadi@islam.org

Goodword Press, 1 Nizamuddin West Market, New Delhi 110 013, India
Tel: 91-11-461-1128. Fax: 91-11-469-7333 and 464-7980
Web site: www.alrisala.org E-mail: skhan@vsnl.com

Type set, Printed, and Published by Goodword Press, New Delhi

CONTENTS

PREFACE AND ACKNOWLEDGMENTS
TO THIRD EDITION

Since the Second English edition of this book was published, its Arabic translation has been published in three editions besides my other books. I also recorded in Abu Dhabi thirty-six episodes of a TV-video program, "Qur'an for Exploring the Earth and Heavens from Space." This is an extended version of this book; it utilizes still pictures and film strips from NASA. It might be released in late 1999 for viewing on TV stations and video cassettes, *in sha Allah.* Since 1996 we have also revived the Institute of Islamic Sciences, Technology, and Development. IISTD promotes Islamization of the natural and social sciences, and technology, through the secular colleges and universities of North America in particular by utilzing their unique facilities. Students are urged to have an Islamic discipline-oriented second major besides their secularized first major. In this edition I have also added three essays on the geophysical sciences: "Light and Vision"; "Lightning: Benefits and Harm"; and "Altitude Sickness." Their focus, as with many of the NASA pictures, is on the earth.

The goal of the above efforts is Islamization of all knowledge, education systems, and careers. This is the most important but neglected Islamic duty of our times; it is also a Muslim necessity, and the need of mankind as discussed in the longest essay of this book. Islamization of the "two cultures,"—the ideological and technological—requires reformation of the Muslim religious mentality. The primary source for Islamization is the Qur'an, through

(1) its ideological or philosophical (*shari'ah*) truths of metaphysics, epistemology, rationalism, ethics and values, etc., and (2) the fact that the rational (*'aqaliyyah*) Truths of the sciences and technology, whether economics or astronomy, are also the creation of God (*khalq Allah*), tradition of God (*sunnah* of *Allah*), and signs of God (*ayat* of *Allah*). Secularism, by definition, excludes God Almighty and His guidance revealed in the Qur'an; Islamization is, thus, de-secularization of the two cultures. Islamization includes assimilation of the Truths of the rational sciences, *al-'ulum al-'aqaliyyah*, developed by modern secularized non-Muslims and their Muslim "blind imitators." Islam is *din al-haq*, the system or way of Truth, and the *din* of God (*din Allah*, Qur'an 3:83; 24:2; etc.). An example of such assimilation is this book which Islamizes the knowledge of modern secular scientists, technologists, and NASA explorations. When the early Muslims followed the Qur'an and the true *sunnah* of Prophet Muhammad, they developed and maintained "world intellectual supremacy" and "hegemony" of the two cultures during at least six centuries, from the first to eighth centuries A.H./seventh-fourteenth A.C. centuries. The purpose of this book is to motivate Muslims in particular to pursue again the Islamic sciences and technology for their own good and the benefit of mankind.

My research and publications projects, and now the Institute of Islamic Sciences, Technology, and Development too, continue to benefit from the help and support of individuals and institutions mentioned in the acknowledgments to the first and second editions. I add to that list the following with deep gratitude:

USA: Islamic Society of North America; Islamic Circle of North America; Mr. Abdul Salam Quraishi, President, Sysorex International; and Prof. Roger Noll, Public Policy Program, Stanford University.

Saudi Arabia: Prince Abdul Aziz bin Fahad, Special Advisor to the Custodian of the Two Holy Mosques, King Fahad bin Adul Aziz; Prince Sultan bin Salman, Space Explorer on "Discovery 5," June 1985; Shaikh Abdul Rahman al-Jeraisy, Chairman, Al-Jeraisy Group; and Engineer Adel Muhammad Fakeih, Chairman, Savola Company.

UAE: Mr. Mohammad al-Fandi Al-Mazroui, Chairman, Al-Mazroui Group; Engineer Bushara Makkawi; Mr. Adnan Haddad, TV-Video Programs Producer, Arab Information and Public Relations Co.; Mr. Naeem Qavi, Eagle Star International Life; and Dr. Asim Ghoshal.

Kuwait: Mr. Fuad M. Al-Juma, Director, Kuwait Science Club; Mr. Abdulla Ali Mutawa, Social Reform Society; Prof. Sabah al-Fedaghi and Prof. Moosa al-Mazeedi, Committee of Kuwait Friends of IISTD, the Institute of Islamic Sciences, Technology, and Development.

Syria: Prof. Mahmood Akkam, Ms. Sumayyah Zaituni, and Abdul Baset Ibrahim, *Fussilat* for Studies, Translation and Publication.

India: My publishers, the Goodword Press and particularly Saniyasnain Khan who has devoted his life to promote Islam; and Ms Susan Brady Maitra, who proof-read this book and made valuable editorial suggestions.

Astronomical Sciences in the Qur'an, the first edition of

this book, was initially sponsored by a Saudi benefactor and was to comprise other disciplines besides astronomy. This project could not be completed, and he wished to remain anonymous. However, "...God does not fail to requite the doers of good" (Qur'an 9:120).

I owe my best thanks to a constant Saudi supporter of my research and publications, and now the Institute of Islamic Sciences, Technology, and Development too. He insists on remaining anonymous according to the ideal prescribed by God Almighty: "And do not bestow favors to obtain increase, but for [the cause of] your Sustainer be persevering" (Qur'an 74:6-7). Therein, indeed, is "good in this world and good in the Hereafter" (Qur'an 2:201).

S. Waqar Ahmed Husaini

Cupertino, California
Jamad al-Akhir 1420
September 1999

PREFACE AND ACKNOWLEDGMENT TO THE SECOND EDITION

The main goals of this book are to invite and motivate Muslims and non-Muslims to study the Qur'an, and use its guidance in development and application of Islamic science and technology. This book is another proof that the Qur'an could not have been produced by any individual or culture before or since Muhammad, peace and the blessing of God Almighty be upon him. The correlation of Qur'anic verses presented here with the findings of modern astronomical sciences should convince any rational and sincere person that the Qur'an is the infallible revelation of God Almighty. Such persons should be Muslim believers and practitioners of the Qur'an in its holistic and integrated context of both rational knowledge and philosophical truth. Most of the "good Muslims" are not such holistic or *tawhidic* Muslims; they are guilty of a serious deviation (*tahrif*) called reduction or restriction (*takhsis*) by Imam al-Ghazali. They have restricted the Qur'an and Islam to the "five pillars," personal morality, etc., and excluded from them Islamic natural sciences and technology, Islamic economics, etc. This book calls upon Muslims to make the Qur'an the source for continuous education and application of all kinds of Islamic sciences and Islamic technology. The basic purpose of this book is, therefore, to bring about a radical paradigm-shift in the religious mentality of reductionist Muslims (*takhsisiyyun*). It presents epistemological ideas and methodology to Islamize the natural and applied sciences, and technology, and the underlying Muslim intellectual and cultural mentalities. Some of these issues are discussed in detail in the first two chapters.

I thank the U.S. National Aeronautical and Space Administration (NASA) for use of their photographs and other information. I have continued to receive the support and encouragement of those mentioned in my Acknowledgements to the first edition. I add to them the following, some of whom are also making endeavors to translate and publish this book in other languages besides English: Dr. Ibrahim H. al-Quayyid and Dr. Maneh H. al-Johany, World Assembly of Muslim Youth, Riyadh; Dr. Darwish M. al-Gobaisi, International Foundation for Water Science and Technology, Abu Dhabi; Mr. Ahsan Rashid, Jeddah; Dr. Hashim M. Mahdi, Muslim World League, Makkah; Haji Abdul Aziz Hashim, Dubai; Mr. "Buhary" K. Muhammad, Al-Amana, and Care Institute, Abu Dhabi; Dr. Mahmood 'Akkam, *Fussilat* for Studies, Translation and Publication, Aleppo; and Dr. M. Zaki Kirmani, The Muslim Association for the Advancement of Science, Aligarh, India. These brothers and many others have made my work possible by answering the call of God with their sincere protestation: "And no reward do I ask of you for it; my reward rests with none but the Sustainer of the worlds" (Qur'an 26:127).

S. Waqar Ahmed Husaini

Cupertino, California
Jamad al-Thani 1416
October 1995

PREFACE AND ACKNOWLEDGMENTS
TO THE FIRST EDITION

I owe my most gratitude to my Saudi Arabian benefactors who have been supporting my research, publications, and promotion programs in Islamization of the sciences and technology. They have supported my work financially, mobilized support, and patronized it with a generosity of spirit which, I believe, is unique to the noble people of Saudi Arabia and its institutions. The later are both private firms and those sponsored by the government of the Kingdom of Saudi Arabia. My latter benefactor has been the Muslim World League, one of its agencies is the Commission on Scientific Signs in the Qur'an and Sunnah which undertakes and promotes modern scientific explanations of the Qur'an like what I have presented in this work. I offer my most humble and sincere tribute to the unique nobility of Saudi people and institutions by identifying some of their characteristics. This is my duty in the spirit of a Saying/*hadith* of Prophet Muhammad, peace and the blessings of God Almighty be upon him: He who is not thankful to people is not thankful to God.

Qur'an and Sunnah must pervade the Saudi Arabian environment and institutions. Nowhere in the world are they as intensively studied and promoted, I believe, as in Saudi Arabia through the curricula and courses in schools and universities, the electronic and printed media, and the activities of private and public institutions. Nowhere does one find turned into mosques at prayer times even the street corners, hallways of shopping centers, and sides of highways in the desert, as in this *mahbatul wahy* (the land where the Qur'an was revealed). No wonder, then, that the Saudi people and its institutions embody some of the noblest ethical qualities of the Qur'an and Prophet Muhammad's model behavior (Sunnah). They include the young in Saudi schools and universities, those who obtained Ph.D. degrees from U.S.A. after their Islamic acculturation in the Saudi environment, and those of the older generations who were brought up in and represent the Saudi traditions. A measure of their nobility and generous spirit is their treatment with kindness, forgiveness, and marked dignity even those who oppose or offend them. The Saudi Government has been the most generous in the world in providing foreign aid as a percentage of its GNP through international agencies and little known unpublicized channels. The Saudi private assistance provided to various Islamic causes is known only to God Almighty; the Saudis really give with one hand what the other hand does not know. They oppose public mention of their giving and goodness; according to the ideals of Islamic ethics, they merely want the rewards to be added undiminished to the scale of their good deeds on the Day of Recknoning. I mention two such persons, who are representatives of my benefactors, without their consent. One is Shaikh Ahmad Salah Jamjoom whom I first encountered in the 1970s through the World Conferences on Muslim Education. He was Chairman of their Organizing Committee, and a moving spirit in our contemporary movement for Islamization of knowledge and education. His indefatigable work for Islam through aid and deeds rather than mere words is one of his best precepts that all Muslims should follow. The other is Professor Abdullah Omar Naseef, formerly both the President of King Abdul Aziz University and Secretary General of the Muslim World League, my chief patron off and on for twenty years through my various vicissitudes, a partner in our intellectual and institutional work on Islamization of science and technology, and an intimate friend ever since we were graduate students at Stanford University, 1964-65.

My Preface should bring out our strong feelings to remove Muslim backwardness and to develop Islamic science and technology for the sake of Muslims and mankind. A Saudi institution which utilizes the leadership of young Saudi professors and other concerned volunteers, to mobilize similar young Muslims around the world, is the World Assembly of Muslim Youth. I owe many thanks to WAMY's officers and administration in Riyadh for their help and encouragement. WAMY and similar associations of young Muslim intellectuals world-wide are providing creative and constructive responses for Islamic renaissance and Muslim development even in environments where there is despair and discouragement. I am hopeful, through my experiences with the Islamic spirit and potentials of such Muslim youth around the world, that Islamization of all knowledge, science and technology in particular, will be a growing trend of our times.

I also acknowledge with gratitude the benefits I have been receiving from two other institutions: American Islamic College, Chicago, particularly Professor Asad Husain (President) and Mr. Waris Cowlas (Chairman,

Board of Directors); and Stanford University, California, which has provided me its facilities and association of its scholars, as a Visiting Scholar since 1986. One who stands out most among the latter, an embodiment for me of Christian love and benevolence, is Dr. Lewis W. Spitz, who retired this year as William R. Kenan University Professor, and Professor of History.

Last but not the least, I owe an unremittable debt of gratitude to my family. It is hard that those whom I love most, and are nearest to me, should suffer most because I chose the hard life of a scholar and protagonist of Islamic science. God knows best what is evident and what is hidden. I turn to Him for forgiveness and mercy, and I beseech Him to open up the hearts of people with kindness so that they may continue to support my work.

S. Waqar Ahmed Husaini

Cupertino, California
Rajab 1415/December 1994

INTRODUCTION TO
PHOTOGRAPHS AND IMAGES

The Teacher Resource Centre, NASA Ames Research Center, Moffet Field, California, provided information for the photographs and images presented and described here. I am thankful for these resources of NASA, the National Aeronautical and Space Administration, U.S.A.

The Qur'anic verses with the photographs deal with the scientific, metaphysical and ethical aspects of the phenomena and planetary bodies. They illustrate *tawhid* which "integrates" all creation with the concept of God to develop Islamic theoretical and applied philosophy of science and technology. The Qur'an is God's Guidance, Criteria, etc. about the truth of science and philosophy. A majority of the illustrations represent the application of space science and technology to studies of our earth's geology, geomorphology, stratosphere, biosphere, hydrology, forest resources, and man-made and natural environmental problems.

God Almighty commands us to see, observe, use the senses and reason, even travel in space to gain knowledge of planetary bodies, and use His signs *(ayat)* as Islamic science, technology, and ethics to manage the Earth. The years since 1959 began a golden age of exploration of the solar system, and the earth from space. However, it was the non-Muslims who were able and willing to mobilize their secularized scholars *(ulama)* and economic resources, and their secularized sciences and technology, to gain understanding (*fiqh*) and knowledge (*'ilm*) through the electronic "sights" and other "senses" of automated spacecraft. We Muslims have been in recent centuries a "blinded people or civilization" (*qawmun 'amin*, Qur'an 7:64); they are "deaf, dumb and blind, so they have no rational knowledge" (Qur'an 2:171), because we have turned our backs on His observable and knowable signs. The early Muslims, on the other hand, had world intellectual supremacy, hence power and dignity, for at least six centuries from the second-eighth centuries A.H. (eighth-fourteenth centuries A.D.) because they followed the Qur'an and the good pattern (*uswatun hasanah*) of Prophet Muhammad.

The purpose of this book, text and illustrations, is to divert both Muslims and non-Muslims to the Qur'an to "Islamize knowledge" and apply it as Islamic science and technology. Secularized peoples and secularized knowledge are a curse for the earth and mankind: "... and any for whom God has appointed no light, there is no light" (Qur'an 24:40).

The list of photographs is given below:

CHAPTER 1

Islamization of Science and Technology: An Islamic Duty and Muslim Necessity

Introduction

Contemporary Muslims all over the world are backward, and have been so for some centuries, in science, technology and, therefore, in many sectors of social and economic development. This has implications not only for Muslims worldwide, who constitute over one fifth of mankind; it has profound impact on the relations of Muslims with their neighbors in their own and neighboring countries. Thus Muslim backwardness is and has been a threat to domestic, regional and international peace and welfare. Efforts undertaken in recent centuries and decades to remove and reverse this backwardness have been a failure; all these efforts have been through secularism in various forms such as the Western, Marxist, and other ethnic and nationalist adaptations. The standard practice has been to impart some "Islamic education," and plenty of dialectical theology;

all other disciplines, the "modern" natural and social sciences, are learnt and practiced in a secular ideological world-view. Secularized knowledge, imbibed by Muslims or enforced upon them, either made them avoid all knowledge other than "Islamic studies"; or they accepted it superficially to become mediocre imitators of secular cultures and enterprises. This has created a dichotomy: the existence of two strongly contrasting and conflicting cultures. A Muslim's material or technological culture is under constant attack from his stronger, self-indicting, Islamic ideological culture. The basic solution for these problems and Muslim backwardness is to remove this dualism and dichotomy by Islamization of all knowledge. Muslim material and ideological cultures must be integrated under a holistic Islamic worldview. This book is an effort in that direction through Islamization of science and technology: providing the Islamic worldview for the astronomical sciences.

Many issues and problems come up due to real or apparent conflict between the Qur'anic revelation and rational knowledge, and specifically in pursuing astronomical sciences in the light of the Qur'an[1]. The basic generalizations and conclusions in interpretation of Qur'anic verses through modern scientific thought can not be repeated in each essay in this book; these are discussed briefly here to develop and present the methodology for Islamization of science and technology.

Mankind is suffering due to backwardness in science and technology; this may be because they are unsound and inappropriate in theory and application; and it may be the result of wrong ethics and values in science and technology.

Islamization of science and technology will impact upon and solve these problems of all mankind rather than just the Muslims.

The Rise and Decline of Medieval Islamic Sciences, and Modern Muslim Predicament.

The Qur'an was revealed to Prophet Muhammad in about twenty-two years (13 B.H. - A.H. 11/A.D. 610-32). Within about a hundred years, by the middle of the second century A.H. (eighth A.D. century), the Muslims had achieved world "intellectual supremacy." This is according to the data first presented in 1927 by George Sarton in his m onum entalw ork, *An Introduction to the History of Science.* Muslims of the medieval Islamic civilization had world hegemony in science and learning for about 500-600 years, during the second to seventh centuries A.H. (eighth to thirteenth centuries A.D.). What were those ideas, beliefs, principles, and policies in the Qur'an, first exemplified by Prophet Muhammad in his *Traditions,* and of Islamic culture of those times, which brought about this supremacy so fast and maintained it for so long?

Near Eastern and European Christianity went through various stages and responses in facing this intellectual supremacy, in assimilating Muslim science and learning, and eventually transcending it. Most Western historians believe that the decline of Muslim science occurred in the seventh century A.H./thirteenth century A.D.; however, Seyyed Hossein Nasr believes that the "decay" of the sciences among Muslims occurred from the eleventh and twelfth centuries A.H. (1600-1800 A.D.) onwards. There is no doubt that the medieval Muslim World experienced during the seventh-eighth centuries A.H. (thirteenth-fourteenth centuries A.D.), under waves of Mongol-Tartar invasion, the destruction of countries and mass killings the like of which has not been found in the history of mankind. The sixth-seventh centuries A.H. (twelfth-thirteenth centuries A.D.) are known for the Crusades which too contributed to the disruption of Muslim culture. However, these external factors were preceded by, and the consequences of, internal changes in the Muslim cultural mentality. The latter led to intellectual decadence, decline of science and technology, moral and material weakness, loss of power, and thus military and political defeats[2].

However, major efforts to revive science and promote development also started in the twelfth A.H. /eighteenth century A.D. in Muslim countries of the Ottoman world-empire under the impact of the West. This was through various strategies of borrowing, transfer, and assimilation applied to knowledge and education, science and technology, industry and economic growth. Much later, some of the most strenuous efforts for development, through international aid and cooperation never before seen in the history of mankind, were started by Muslims following the end of the Second World War. But whether one compares with war-ravaged Japan, Germany, and Russia, or the newly-developed countries like Singapore and South Korea, Taiwan and Hong Kong, we do not find now any Muslim country comparable to them in such development. One can see also the relative educational and technological backwardness of Muslims, in comparison with the Hindus, whether they live in the Himalayan subcontinent or have migrated to Europe and North America[3]

What are the primary reasons for this relative lack of excellence in science, technology, and development among Muslims in various external environments, favorable or challenging, in Muslim majority or minority countries? What different ideological solutions were tried and why did they not succeed with Muslims the way these ideologies of development seem to have worked with non-Muslims? Most important of all, what were the characteristics of the indigenous intellectual and cultural changes that caused the decay and decline of science and technology among Muslims, and continue to thwart all efforts to revive them?

My basic conclusion is that Muslims need a systematic and comprehensive "Islamization" of all knowledge, the sciences and technology as well as the social sciences and humanities. This is a prerequisite for Muslim development. The efforts in recent centuries and decades for technological development of Muslims failed because the worldviews associated with these efforts were non-Islamic and un-Islamic; the failure of these efforts was the failure of secularism, Westernization, Marxianization, and other philosophies of development. Islam and the process of Islamization are not opposed to imitation and borrowing *per se*; they fully endorse imitation and borrowing, but on Islamic terms and conditions. It is impossible for Muslims, even if they are weak in traditional Islamic beliefs and practice, to borrow and imitate from, assimilate, and excel in any field of knowledge that is rooted in and raised upon un-Islamic worldviews. This is based on certain principles of social dynamics presented, for example, by Pitirim A. Sorokin[4].

The basic idea is that a living and dynamic system rejects the implantation of those foreign "systems of meanings" or values, including the worldviews of science and technology, which are in opposition to its own primary system of meanings. Superior values must triumph over inferior values in the long run. Thus Islam is incompatible with secularism, and its other derivatives like Westernism and Marxism. The distinctly un-Islamic philosophy and thought-content of disciplines repels Muslims from acquiring secularized knowledge. Secularism rejects or at least ignores religion because it claims that all religions, including Islam, are opposed to the pursuit of human welfare through reason, science, humanism, etc. Secularism has been accepted by those who found that their own scriptures (sources of their primary system of meanings) were incompatible with the principles of scientific exploration, experimentation and reason. The triumph of secularism over Christianity, Hinduism, and other religions is fully understandable to Muslims. However, Muslims find no such incompatibility and, therefore, have no need of secularism that is valid for other religions. The Qur'an in particular, and the Islamic intellectual legacy in general, pre-empts the critique by secularism that is valid for other religions. Thus the secularist critique of religion in the context of the Bible, the content of Christian thought, the Christian cultural ethos, and the Western historical experience may be quite valid. But it is not so for the Qur'an in particular, and Islam in general. The basic postulates and goals of secularism confirm and support the claims of the Qur'an. Muslims also recognize that secularists are guilty of a massive hypocrisy because they merely seek to avoid and bypass religion; they should either accept a religion or reject it according to secularism's criteria of reason, science, etc. Secularists will find then that Islam is different.

This work on interpretation of the Qur'anic verses on astronomical science shows that the Qur'an, on the one hand, and reason and the experimental sciences on the other are basically in conformity with each other. However, the limits and undemonstrable speculations of science, a distinction between its "facts" and "theories," the relativity of human thought, etc., must also be recognised. Similarly, human understanding of the Qur'an is also fallible, changing, and subject to similar other constraints.

Succinctly then, the backwardness of Muslims is due to the secular, Western, and Marxist worldviews of science and technology which have made them unacceptable to Muslims. Islamization of science and technology, which is their pursuit through an Islamic worldview, will be the successful ideology of development for Muslims just as it was from the first to about the seventh or eleventh centuries A.H. (seventh to thirteenth or seventeenth centuries A.D.). It should be noted too, as demonstrated by the essays in this book, that Islamization also includes assimilation of all compatible human thought, religious or secular. Islamization is a method and process by which the contents of any science or field of knowledge are affirmed and borrowed if they are found to be compatible with the Qur'an regardless of the non-Muslim sources of that knowledge. The birth and rapid development of Islamic thought in the first-second centuries A.H./seventh-eighth centuries A.D., particularly in the "natural or rational sciences," such as the natural sciences and technology, is a testimony to the principles and processes of Islamization through selective borrowing. These were taken from the Qur'an, codified as the basic principles (*qawa'id*) of Islamic law or the *Shari'ah*, and applied universally. The backwardness of Muslims in recent centuries and decades shows that a similar Islamization through both borrowing and innovation, and the development of a distinct and dynamic Islamic scientific worldview, did not take place.

Islamic Science and Technology, and Islamization of Knowledge

Islam is based on the Qur'anic concept of God. God is the *rab* (Sustainer, Nourisher, Maintainer, Developer, Manager, etc.) of the universe; He is the *rab* of the laws with which He manages nature; and it is His ethics with which He governs the heavens and the earth. The Qur'anic concept and definitions of God, His "names" or characteristics, and its other special terms can be used to define Islamic science and technology. Islamic science is, for example, God's laws of nature; it is God's will which created the universe; and it is the laws by which God operates and manages the solar system. To impute to God the creation and management of the universe is Islamization of science. By contrast, the personification of "nature" as the creator of the universe and operator of the geophysical sciences is secularization of science; this is a negation and rejection of God, or *Kufr* The evaluation and assessment of science and technology by Qur'anic or Islamic ethics and laws is also Islamization

31

of science and technology. The basic point is that science and technology do not, and can not, exist and operate in a vacuum of values. Explicitly or implicitly they are valid within a worldview, whether it is a religious or a secular "system of meanings." Science and technology are born, developed, and operate within a system of philosophical sciences: metaphysics, logic, epistemology, ethics (including law), aesthetics, etc. These systems could be Islamic, Western, Marxist-Leninist, or any secular, religious, or mythological system of philosophical sciences. We may have, thus, Islamic environmental laws, and U.S. environmental laws which are a part of the secular Western system. Many specific Islamic and U.S. environmental laws may be similar or even identical due to various causes and reasons. A most important reason is that, according to Islamic epistemology, natural reason that has not been perverted by cultural factors leads to identity with Islamic thought; and that is because God has made man by nature both rational and ethically good.

A discussion of Islamic science must begin with the concept of *tawhid*. It means oneness, unity and unification and holism. God is one; therefore, the source of all truths is one which is God and His will or laws. The truths or laws revealed in the Qur'an about nature and ethics, and the laws by which God operates nature and the universe also can not contradict each other. They are both God's creation, and so can not contradict each other. The Qur'an and nature, or the whole universe, are the two "Books" of one God. *Tawhid* also requires that science, or any discipline, must incorporate the truths of the philosophical sciences as well as those of the rational or physical sciences. There can not be any contradiction between the two, the Qur'an and science, because truth confirms truth. Any conflict or contradiction between the knowledge derived from the Qur'an and pure reason can not be real; it must be merely an apparent conflict due to human error and weakness in man's reasoning , his assumptions, his instruments and methods, etc. It is man's responsibility to remove his errors, and reconcile the conclusions derived from the two sources of knowledge. *Tawhid* requires the deliberate use of both the Qur'an and, on the other hand, reason and nature to discover, develop and utilize Islamic science and technology.

In the early centuries Muslims had a Qur'anic unitary or holistic (*tawhidic*) concept of knowledge (*'ilm*). Every valid discipline, vocation, or "science" is an *'ilm* which has its origin in the Qur'an in a general or specific sense. Every *'ilm* has a "rational" part which is knowable by all human beings since God has made them all capable of it through their "natural reason." The other part of an *'ilm* is value-oriented or ideological; it is based on a "tradition" (any *shari'ah*) such as a religion or a secular belief-system. The integration or unification of these two parts is *tawhid*. These parts are called the rational, *'aqaliyyah*, and the belief system or traditional, *shar'iyyah*. All disciplines or vocations were brought under the Islamic worldview in the early centuries through such *tawhid* or integration. Muslims should seek the knowledge and application of all disciplines, in the natural and social sciences, as an Islamic duty (*fard*) and necessity. The more and better they know an *'ilm* by knowing God's will or laws concerning it in the physical and ethical realms, they are to that extent true and good Muslims; due to the causality of God's immutable laws of that *'ilm* they deserve both "worldly" benefits and rewards in the hereafter. Thus God's laws concerning physics or economics are both physical or rational, and ethical. There is Islamic justification, necessity, obligation, and content for science and technology as Islamic knowledge. There is no separation and differentiation between the religious sciences, and the secular or worldly sciences. This would constitute the worst Islamic sin, *shirk*, or association of gods with God by asserting that somebody other than God is the source and creator of the physical and ethical laws concerning the universe put forth by the secular sciences, and that God has no jurisdiction over them. God can not be excluded from the "secular" sciences. With such a living and operational Islamic cultural mentality and epistemology, there was no possibility of neglecting science and technology, of their decay among Muslims, and of Muslim backwardness in their knowledge and application.

However, a paradigm shift and deviation took place gradually in Muslim concepts of Islam, Islamic knowledge and education, Islamic duty (*fard*), and the whole Muslim cultural mentality along with the orientation of Muslim institutions and behavioral patterns. This may be illustrated with two examples.

First, long before the decay of Muslim science and technology became obvious, it was noticed and diagnosed by the Imam al-Ghazali. He is one of the greatest Islamic scholars of all times, and one of the most influential intellectuals in the history of mankind. Within forty years of his death in A.H. 505/A.D. 1111, most of his books had been translated into Latin. They most profoundly influenced the Christian scholastics who absorbed his thought. His ideas were transmitted to generations of Europeans who studied them in the new universities of Europe patterned on Muslim models; and this initiated the renaissance of Europe and the reformation of Christianity. In his *Book of Knowledge (Kitab al-'ilm)*, Imam al-Ghazali pointed out the deviation (*tahrif*) of Muslims from the Qur'an and true Islam. Reductionism, *takhsis,* was one such major deviation. For example, the word *fiqh* in Arabic and the Qur'an means understanding, a science, any or all knowledge in the holistic sense; *fiqh* was reduced to mean only Islamic law. Gradually Islamic *fiqh* or knowledge was confined to only Islamic personal law.

Second, the origins of this reductionism may be traced to a gradual perversion of Islamic epistemology through Muslim classification of the sciences (*'ulum*). In the beginning, perhaps quite rightly, knowledge or the sciences were divided based on their sources and the methods of knowing them. The sciences derived from a "tradition" or religion were called the positive (*wad'iyyah*) or the *shar'iyyah* sciences; they were specific to a way or tradition (*shara'a*), such as the Islamic or the *Shar'iyyah* sciences. The sciences which were knowable by all mankind, based on man's natural reason (*'aql*) and experience, were called the natural or rational (*tabi'iyyah, 'aqliyyah*) sciences. The early Muslims freely borrowed these universal "rational" sciences and technology from the intellectual legacy of non-Muslim civilizations; they adopted these from the legacies of pre-

Qur'anic or *jahiliyyah* Arabs, the Byzantines, the Sassanid or Persian, the Greek, the Indian Hindu-Buddhist, etc. They undertook their transfer and assimilation through Islamization, or an Islamic value-assessment. Such evaluation led the Muslims to separate astronomy from astrology, physics from metaphysics, the mathematical sciences from numerology and palmistry, medicine from magic and miracle mongering, chemistry from alchemy, and history from hearsay and fables; in short knowledge based on proof (*burhan*) was cleansed from mythology, superstition, and mere speculation (*zann*). However, gradually in later centuries, and as they exist now, the rational (*'aqliyyah*) and the religious (*shar'iyyah*) became two separate and parallel systems of knowledge and education. As Ibn Khaldun (d.A.H. 732 / A.D. 1406) pointed out in his *Muqaddimah*, there developed further a confusion in the methods of knowing, the scope and domain, subject-matter, goals, etc., of these two classes of knowledge. More havoc was caused in Muslim civilization by the creation and development of pseudo-Islamic sciences like Muslim mysticism (*Sufism*), dialectical metaphysics, and speculative theology.

Muslims got so engrossed in these pseudo-sciences during the recent centuries of their decline that science and technology were made irrelevant and unnecessary. They wanted to solve all problems through Sufi psychic exercises, intercession of saints through their prayers and offerings at their graves, etc. The worst perversion was in the use and misuse of the Qur'an. Muslims began to use Qur'anic verses as talisman and amulets, often hung around the neck, dispensed by "saints" and "friends of God" (*awliya' Allah*) to solve any number of scientific, economic, social, and other problems. Muslims sought to suspend and circumvent God's laws of the natural and social sciences, and causality in general, by such uses of Qur'anic verses! In the non-Arab countries Muslims read the Arabic Qur'an without any knowledge of the Arabic language. Chanting of the Qur'an for psychic pleasure developed as a highly respected art, encouraged also by vested interests, while Qur'anic thought ceased to be used in economics, politics, or the sciences. Qur'anic verses were being used for miraculous effects and expectations. The Qur'an was not being used as a guidance and starting point to gain rational understanding or *fiqh* of all disciplines, and to develop them within and through the Qur'anic worldview; and the Qur'an was not being used to evaluate and assess all knowledge through Qur'anic ethics and values. The Qur'an began to be read by the bedside of the dying to invoke "blessings" instead of being used in the classroom, the market, and the astronomical observatory. Thus the ideas and values of the Qur'an, and the principles of *tawhid*, were being violated and abandoned. While this kind of religion continues to flourish among Muslim masses nowadays, Islamic reform movements in many countries have been opposing it with some success, yet without presenting the alternatives of Islamization of knowledge and their application in all disciplines and behavioral culture.

The reductionist and deviationist concept of "Islamic" knowledge and education, "Islamic studies," *fiqh*, etc. is fully entrenched in the Muslim cultural and religious mentality and Muslim institutions. For example, in recent centuries and decades, and nowadays even in the newly established or the old reformed "Islamic universities," Islamic law or *fiqh* is restricted to Muslim family and personal law; the faculties of law in the secularized universities deal with the full scope and diversity of law. Nobody believes in "Islamic *fiqh*" as Islamic knowledge about any and all the sciences and disciplines. The "Islamic" schools and universities, traditional and "modern," systematically exclude in their curricula the natural and applied sciences, technology, most of the social sciences, and even the humanistic sciences; and those who do teach them do so from a secular perspective as "non-Islamic studies." Their "Islamic studies" cover just a few subject areas, and are restricted to some outdated humanistic studies; and the methods and content of their teaching may be poor and defective qualitatively, just like their teachers. Their graduates, who become "Islamic scholars," claim to be experts in giving the Islamic explanation or exegesis (*tafsir*) of the Qur'an. However, their system of "Islamic education" is restricted or reductionist from even the primary school level; their curricula makes them ignorant of the natural sciences, anything technical or technology, and even the social sciences in the contemporary or "modern" concept. These "Islamic scholars" are made by their curricula and education system incapable of giving any technical explanation, *tafsir*, of Qur'anic verses related to contemporary natural and social sciences. This is far removed from the Muslim scholarship of the early centuries when the Qur'anic verses were the motivation and inspiration for Islamic intellectual initiatives, innovations, and world leadership in every branch of knowledge and its application. The "Islamic scholar," then, was second to none in any discipline. There is ample evidence to prove the assertion that there are powerful forces within and outside the systems and institutions of contemporary "Islamic studies" who want to prevent the universalization of Islamic studies and the Islamization of all knowledge.

However, there is now a growing awareness of the defects of this "traditional" system of Islamic education and Muslim culture, and the dichotomy between such Islamic and secular studies and their institutions. Hence efforts are being made in some quarters for Islamization of all knowledge. These were started particularly in the 1970s in many countries of the world, where Muslims are in a majority or minority, and in both Eastern and Western countries. This chapter is not the place to review the many trends and efforts in Islamization of knowledge, or of science and technology particularly, or to point out their strength or inadequacy. It is sufficient to emphasize the Islamic necessity and the pragmatic need to expand, accelerate, and intensify such efforts.

Towards Islamization of Science and Technology

The Qur'an is the Book of "guidance" (Qur'an 2:185; 17:9; etc.) for mankind. It is the Book of God that throws "light" on all the key words, topics, sciences and disciplines dealt with in its 6226 verses. The frequency of verses on any key word or discipline must show their importance in the sight of God. On the other hand, the lack of repetition could point out that the particular subject is definitive and does not need much discussion. Thus from among "the five pillars" of Islam, there are only eight verses on Hajj, the Pilgrimage to Makkah, and only six verses on fasting in the month of Ramadan. My major works show that there are about 900 verses on "Water Resources Sciences and Engineering" in the Qur'an and nearly 1400 verses on "Economics" in the Qur'an. However, the Qur'an is not a textbook or encyclopedia on water resources or economics either. The most important objectives of this work are summarized below.

There is proof in the Qur'an, as claimed in it, that it is indeed an infallible Book revealed for mankind by God Almighty.

> Will they not, then, try to understand this Qur'an? Had it issued from any but God, they would surely have found in it many an inner contradiction! (Qur'an 4:82, n97, trans. Muhammad Asad)

The Qur'an was revealed to an unlettered man, Muhammad, when he was forty years old. The essays presented here show that the Qur'anic verses deal with some facts and ideas on astronomical sciences which were not known to and could not have been even imagined by Muhammad, his contemporaries, or the world civilizations of those times; the same can be said about verses on many other sciences. This fact stands out in the verses and every fact or theory in modern astronomy related to them. Once a person is convinced by these proofs of the Divine Origin of the Qur'an, then he or she would be ready to view and use the Qur'an as the Book of God's guidance, light, wisdom, etc. All the descriptive words used in the Qur'an, to describe the Qur'an, become very significant for the purposes and subject of this work.

Non-Muslims, and Muslims who do not have sufficient knowledge of the Qur'an, would study astronomical sciences in the Qur'an with a different outlook. They might seek conviction on rational grounds to make a commitment to follow Islam. This work could be an introduction and invitation to the Qur'an and Islam for them.

The Qur'an was revealed 1400 years ago, but it is for all peoples now and in the future just as it was for the generations before us. Its terminology, therefore, has to be understood by each generation according to the knowledge of the times. They should not, however, be dogmatic and self-sure about their knowledge. We could try to find out if and how Muslims during the past 1400 years understood the verses which say that the heavens and earth were once, before their creation, "a smoke"; and they will be turned into "a smoke" at the end of time. Modern astronomers believe that our solar system was created from cosmic "dust," or a gas consisting of both radiation and matter; it will become dust again when it burns up and is destroyed like the other "dead" stars now in space. Is this the "smoke" referred to in the Qur'an? The answer to such questions is given in traditional Islamic language expressing Islamic philosophical and scientific doubt: *Wa-Allahu a'lam;* that is, this is our best judgement based on our knowledge now, "and God knows the best."

In the current debate on "Islamic science," there are Muslims who think that we should not give interpretations of the Qur'anic verses on scientific matters because of the uncertainty and progressive nature of scientific thought. They are afraid that when certain scientific "facts" or "theories" are revised or changed, this will disprove and refute the Qur'an, and a Muslim's faith in the Qur'an will be shaken. This is not a good or right argument. It has been universally agreed by Muslims that man's changing and fallible understanding of the Qur'an does not affect its words, which are not changed. Man has an Islamic duty to try to understand the Qur'an despite the fact that the "real or true" meanings are known with certainty only by God. This is called "exerting oneself," or giving *ijtihad*, "an expert opinion or judgement." The important point is that man is under Divine Order to increase his knowledge of these sciences, and to continue to make *ijtihad*. The concept of *ijtihad* must be used for "expert scientific opinion" too as is evident from many verses quoted in the following pages. The explanations, *tafsir*, given on astronomical sciences are such *ijtihad* on the authority of available expert but fallible human knowledge.

Many of the scientific ideas presented here are perhaps of the category of "theories" rather than "facts." A simple "fact" is that we can "see" the sun and the moon. However, even in the Qur'an the commands to "see," "observe" and "travel" are used in extremely complex contexts that may be beyond the capability of man to grasp. This is perhaps a command to form undemonstrable theories with humility, and make certain conclusions. These may be developing a strong belief in God Almighty, preparing ourselves to seek more and more knowledge, and living profoundly rational and ethical Islamic lives. This command to try to see, observe, etc., and make *ijtihad* under conditions of great uncertainty may have many purposes in God's wisdom. An example of this are the verses where the verbs are used in the second person plural imperative form: *Do they not see* (yaraw), *then, how God creates in the first instance, and then brings it forth anew? This, verily, is easy for God! Say: 'You should then travel* (fa-siiruu) *in the earth, and you should observe* (fa-anzuruu) *how He has created in the first instance ...'* (Qur'an 29:19f).

Cosmological and other astronomical theories presented here are also based on certain unprovable and even unknowable premises, that is, presuppositions and assumptions. For example, it is said that cosmological theories, or explantions of the origin and behavior of the universe, are based on the premise that one part of the universe is like any other part having the same "age." The estimates of the age of the universe or its parts, like even a star, are also based on changing premises! The general theory of relativity of Einstein is also a basis for cosmological theories. Einstein's theory itself is based on two premises: no signal can travel faster than the speed of light; and the laws of physics are the same everywhere in the universe. Astronomers realize that the vastness of the universe is incomprehensible and unknowable by man. This brief discussion must make us realize a few things. The fact that the ideas presented by astronomers are based on premises must be kept in mind at all times in the following pages.

We must realize the limits of human reason and the constraints on the sciences. The Qur'anic verses and the scientific ideas presented here must create in any sensible person a greater awe of God Almighty, and belief in the Qur'an as the true Book of God. In it are presented both simple and the most complex cosmological and other astronomical ideas which will always be proven right and can never be disproved. However, the goals of this work are also very sociological. We want to return Muslims to Islamic science and development.

The Qur'an should be used as God's guidance and light to initiate, develop, and utilize "Islamic science and technology." "Islamic sciences," "Islamic religious sciences," "Islamic studies and education," etc. include the Islamic natural sciences and technology; these are by definition inter-disciplinary through the integration (*tawhid*) of science and technology with the social and humanistic sciences. Islamic science and technology is not created by "proving that the Qur'an is right," by citing the intellectual achievements of modern non-Muslim scholars from an encyclopedia. We do not have to "read into" the Qur'an the facts and theories of modern astronomical and other sciences. Muslims must initiate a process and not just reuse the end-products of non-Muslims. In this process of Islamization, there is no place for historical romanticism, xenophobia, blind imitation through excessive veneration for the medieval Muslim legacy or the modern non-Muslim achievements, etc. Muslims should follow the principles and policies of the Muslims and neo-Muslims of the first-second centuries A.H. /seventh-eighth centuries

A.D. They not only used the guidance and light of the Qur'an, and the model behavior of Prophet Muhammad as the "sociologist" of science and technology, and of social change and development; but in relation to the heritage of "mixed" knowledge of the times, they resorted to selective but creative borrowing as well as their own originality and creativity.

Contemporary Muslims must take lessons from the history and sociology of Muslim science of the early centuries. They will then be able to revive their development in all its comprehensiveness. Muslims would then be capable also of inviting all mankind to a God-oriented and Islamic, rather than the "modern" secularized and Godless science and technology. Mankind has lost too much since the intellectual supremacy of Muslims was lost. With that were lost the singular characteristics of Islamic science and civilization which were God-centered, and dominated by moral and ethical considerations. The references given in chapter 2 could lead the reader towards an Islamic and comparative study of these characteristics. These, however, should always be evaluated through the Qur'an since Muslims, their intellectual legacy, and their history are at best a step towards the Qur'an and at worst in conflict with it.

The methodology presented in the following pages for Islamization of science and technology is one such method. It is a simple method, within the capabilities of most Muslims who do not have much knowledge of the Islamic legacy or the history and philosophy of Muslim science and technology. A detailed formulation of Islamization, in a generalized form and particularly suited for the social sciences and humanities, is given in Ismail R. al-Faruqi's *Islamization of Knowledge*. The method that can be followed by each Muslim, within his or her capabilities, is presented in a few steps. (1) With a rudimentary knowledge of Arabic, one must get the key word or words for a topic. (2) All the verses of the Qur'an on these words and their derivatives must be collected by using, for example, Fuad Abdul Baqi, *Al-Mu'jam al-Mufahris lil-Alfaz al-Qur'an al-Karim*, or other concordances. (3) All possible meanings of the key word or words must be studied from Edward W. Lane, *An Arabic English Lexicon*. (4) A reputed translation of the Qur'an must be used while keeping in mind the Arabic text of the Qur'an, and the meanings of the key words. Perhaps the best such translation with notes on key words is by Muhammad Asad, *The Message of the Qur'an*. (5) One must then use an encyclopedia to get the most authoritative knowledge of the subject. (6) One must learn by heart as many verses of the Qur'an as possible on the subject of one's interest. These verses must be used as guidance for daily inspiration, and orientation to develop and use Islamic science in one's own life and profession. (7) This could lead to contributions to Islamic science and technology through further research and publications. Each individual could adapt this method to his or her own needs and capabilities. The simplest step would be for a Muslim to regularly read the Qur'an with an eye on the verses in ones field of work and study.

Notes

[1] *The Message of the Qur'an,* translated and explained by Muhammad Asad (Gibraltar: Dar al-Andalus Ltd., 1980). All references to the Qur'an in this work are to this translation and its notes, referred to as n or nn in the verses cited in the various Articles. I have also taken the liberty of modifying Asad's translations to make it simple or conform with the Arabic text or my needs for use in Islamic science. Asad's notes are important in developing Islamic science through an understanding of the classical Arabic of the Qur'an; his notes often summarize the classical Arabic meanings of the key words occurring in the verses. The serious reader is encouraged to use Asad's original source for English meanings of the Arabic words: Edward W. Lane, *An Arabic-English Lexicon,* 2 vols (Cambridge, England: Islamic Texts Society Trust, 1984; first published in 8 volumes, London: Williams & Northgate, 1863-1893).

[2] S.Waqar Ahmed Husaini, *Islamic Science and Public Policies: Lessons from History of Science* (Kuala Lumpur, 1986; Distributors, London: Islamic Foundation; and Indianapolis: American Trust Publications); and, *Islamic Environmental Systems Engineering: A systems study of environmental engineering, and the law, politics, education, economics, and sociology of science and culture of Islam* (Indianapolis: Amer. Trust publ., and London: Macmillan, 1980), chaps. 3 and 7 on the history and sociology of Islamic sciences and civilization, and their assimilation by Western Christians. The best source to date of this in English is still George Sarton, *An Introduction to the History of Science* (3 vols. in 5; Baltimore: Williams and Wilkins co., 1927-48), esp. 1:6-17, 503, 521, 523, 527, 544, 549, 557f, 599-601, 611, *et passim,* and 2:1-3, 98f, 109, 321-30, 485, 709, 808f, 815, 818. See also, G. Sarton, *The Incubation of Western Culture in the Middle East,* (Washington, D.C.: U.S. Govt. Printing Office, 1952); G. Sarton, "Arabic Science and Learning in the Fifteenth Century: Their Decadence and Fall," in *Homenage a Millas-Vallicrosa* (2 vols, Barcelona: Consejo Superior de Investigaciones Cientificas, 1956); and Mehdi Nakosteen, *History of Islamic Origins of Western Education, AD 800-1350* (Boulder: Univ Colorado Press, 1964). The works of Seyyed Hossein Nasr include, *Islamic Science: An Illustrated Study* (2nd ed.; London: World of Islam Festival Trust, 1976), esp.p.19; and *Science and Civilization in Islam* (Cambridge: Harvard Univ Press, 1968; and Shah Alam, Malaysia: Dewan Pustaka Fajar, 1984). The reader

interested in Islamic science and technology is also encouraged to refer to the *MAAS Journal of Islamic Science* and similar other publications from various countries. *MAAS J.* had published a bibliography of Seyyed Hossein Nasr.

[3] See statistical data and discussions in my "Birth, decline, and rebirth of Islamic science and technology: Indigenous causes of decline, and their remedies," *MAAS J. Islamic Science* (India), 2 (Jan.-June, 1986): 75-91; and *An Islamic Assessment of Development and Belligerence in the Sub-Himalayan Countries: Policy Implications for India, Pakistan, Bangladesh, USA, and Global Development Strategies,* Intl Working Papers Series, I-91-15, Hoover Institution on War, Revolution and Peace, Stanford University, California; July 1991, pp +108, also published as "Environmental development vs military expenditure: An analysis of Muslim countries," *Jour. of Objective Studies* (India), 5 (July 1993): 18-69.

[4] Pitirim A. Sorokin, *Social and Cultural Dynamics* (4 vols. New York: American Book Co., 1937-41) esp. 4:45-95; and Arnold J. Toynbee, "Sorokin's philosophy of history," in *Pitirim A. Sorokin in Review*, P.J. Allen (ed.) (Durham, N.C.: Duke Univ. Press, 1963.

CHAPTER 2

An Introduction to Islamic and Comparative Astronomy, and Related Sciences and Pseudo-Sciences

Definitions

Astronomy has been defined as the study of the stars, planets, and other objects in the universe. Cosmology, in particular, is the study of the structure and formation of the universe, its past and future. The universe includes our earth and everything on it, our solar system, and all the matter, light, and other forms of radiation and energy which have been discovered; thus the universe comprises everything which, based on studies and theories, the scientists believe to be present in space and time.

Modern scientists believe that stars, like our sun, are glowing balls of hot gases made up mainly of hydrogen and helium. Stars shine because atomic energy makes these gases very hot; they produce light and energy until they run out of their hydrogen fuel. The planets, like our moon and Earth, are dark, solid bodies; they get all their light and nearly all their heat from the sun. Constellations are groups of stars within a region of the sky; astronomers have divided the sky into 88 constellations for purposes of mapping.

A galaxy is a system of stars, space dust, and gas which is held together by gravity. Astronomers do not know how many galaxies there are in the universe; they have photographed millions of them. The diameter of a galaxy may be a few thousand to half a million light years. A light year is the distance travelled by light in a year: about 5.88 trillion miles. Light travels at 186,282 miles/second. The Milky Way Galaxy is said to have over 100 billion stars; it is so vast that it is about 100,000 light years across, and about 16,000 light years thick at its center.

Our solar system is a tiny speck located between the upper and lower edges of the Milky Way Galaxy, about 30,000 light years from its center. The solar system comprises one star, which is our sun at its center, and the following objects which all orbit it: nine planets, most of which have their own satellites or moons which travel around them, including our earth and moon; small nebular objects called asteroids; small chunks of iron and rock called meteoroids; meteorites which are meteoroids that fall upon the earth; bodies of dust and frozen gas called comets; and drifting particles and gas called, respectively, interplanetary dust and interplanetary plasma.

The phrases "modern scientists believe," "astronomers believe," etc. are not used often in the book hereafter except to emphasize a speculative, controversial or similar statement. However, all statements of "fact" or "scientific opinion" must be understood to be made on the authority of modern science and scientists. Islamic thought, including Islamic science, requires that we be always aware of the fallibility of our perceived "fact" and "expert opinion" (*ijtihad*); only God Almighty knows the truth without any doubt. This is *Islamic philosophical doubt*. Islamic scholars, from the earliest times, institutionalized this by ending their expert opinions with the phrase, "and God knows the best" (*wa-Allahu a'lam*).

The Qur'an, Knowledge, and *Tawhid*

One of the most important principles of the Qur'an, very much manifest in the Sayings and Life of Prophet Muhamad, is *tawhid* or integration. The Qur'an deals with both the physical sciences and the philosophical or socio-humanistic sciences. *Tawhid* "integrates" them, individually and as "knowledge" itself, into holistic sub-systems or disciplines, and the universal Islamic thought, culture and civilization. The verses cited in the following chapters, and their "scientific" explanations, will also bring out *tawhid*: the integration of the sciences, morality, the Hereafter, etc., often in the same verse. One should not look for or try to obtain "secular astronomy" divorced from God in the Qur'an. Therefore, the Qur'anic verses on astronomy are presented alongwith some of the adjoining verses to preserve their organic oneness or *tawhid*. They provide both the "scientific facts" of astronomy, and the ethics, values, and the "unobservable truths" concerning this world and the Hereafter. The verses are meant only to guide mankind towards pursuing astronomy, cosmology, etc. through their *tawhidic* or rational-ethical, scientific-ethical integrated understanding.

The Qur'an is not a textbook or an encyclopedia on astronomy, or any other subject, not even on the concept of God. Its verses negate whatever comes in the way of the *tawhidic* system of knowledge. In the case of astronomy, directly or indirectly, they negate mythology, superstition, and other pseudo-sciences like astrology. Chapter 4 deals with the negation of astrology in the Qur'an; it points out why and how Muslim energies were directed away from astrology and its epistemic, sociological, and other disastrous consequences, and towards Islamic astronomy: its *tawhidic* or rational-ethical integrated studies. The Muslims did this for many centuries, later on with decreasing creativity, until about the eleventh century A.H./ seventeenth century A.D. and twelfth A.H./ eighteenth A.D. century. While the Muslims were giving up the Islamic scientific method, and the pursuit of natural and even many of the socio-humanistic sciences, the non-Muslim West stepped up the pursuit of knowledge, later on under the secular scientific method.

Borrowing and Assimilation of Medieval Muslim Science and Learning by Non-Muslim Europeans: The Beginning of Modernity

The medieval West comprised both Christian Europe in its so-called Dark Ages, and the Islamic Europe of Spain and Southern Europe (particularly Sicily, and parts of Italy and France). This Islamic Europe both received from the Near East and produced an indigenous Islamic culture on European soil; this intellectual and behavioral Islamic culture was transmitted to the non-Muslim parts of Europe.

European Christianity was, thus, under the full impact of medieval Islamic civilization. Christian Europe had the deepest possible physical and intellectual contacts with Muslims in "European Islam" and the Near East. The intellectual contacts were through direct absorption of Islamic knowledge through works in the Arabic language, and their translations into Latin and other European languages. The European Christians had mastered Arabic language at least as early as the third century A.H./ ninth century A.D.; the Arab Muslims had settled in Spain, etc. first in the second century A.H./eighth century A.D.. The two centuries of the Crusades were marked by brief periods of warfare but long periods of truce and intellectual and cultural communication between Muslims and Christian Europeans in the Muslim lands of the Near East and the Holy Lands. And it was during this period, the sixth century A.H./twelfth century A.D. and seventh century A.H./thirteenth century A.D., that the most strenuous efforts were made in Europe by European Christians, aided by non-Christians like the poly-lingual Jews, to assimilate Islamic intellectual culture.

The dominant activities of these centuries were two: the translation of Islamic works in the sciences and philosophy (including Islamic theological sciences) into Latin and other European languages; and the founding of universities in Christian Europe, patterned after Islamic universities, to assimilate Islamic thought that inundated European peoples and lands. Thus Europe assimilated Islamic thought and culture during the second century A.H./eighth century A.D. to more or less the tenth century A.H./sixteenth century A.D.. This was also a period, more or less, of Islamic intellectual supremacy and dominance, and Muslim political and military power. Through such contacts and conflicts with Islam and Muslims, Christian Europe adopted later on a changed version and only one aspect of *tawhid*; this eventually developed into secularism, and the secular scientific method. However, for many centuries in the beginning, Christian scholars tried to develop "Christian *tawhidic*" sciences, culture, and civilization patterned after their Islamic models. These efforts failed because the Bible in particular, and the ethos of Christianity in general, were incompatible with reason, science, and humanism too. Pitirim A. Sorokin, a great sociologist of culture, classified the main supersystems of culture mentality into the ideational, the sensate, and the idealistic (or balanced or integrated). He defined an idealistic culture as "a harmonious blending together, into one system, of the truths of faith, of reason, and of the senses"; it is the symbiosis of the ideational (an utterly other-worldly) and the sensate culture mentalities.

Sorokin showed that the age of idealistic rationalism lasted in Christian Europe from about the end of the fifth century A.H./eleventh century A.D. to the eighth century A.H./fourteenth century A.D.; and that "the greatest creators" of this idealistic culture were St. Albert the Great and St. Thomas Aquinas, the seventh century A.H./ thirteenth century A.D. Catholic scholastics. Sorokin's idealistic, balanced, or integrated culture mentality is similar generically to the Islamic *tawhidic* culture mentality.

It is outside the scope and purpose of this book to trace the history of the passage of European Christianity and the

West from the Dark Ages to modern intellectual and technological supremacy, from ideationalism to modern secularism through Christian idealistic culture. Similarly, we cannot trace here the general and specific ways, processes, and examples of Western adoption and adaptation, imitation and assimilation, of Islamic natural and social sciences, culture and civilization. That is, the history, causes, and consequences of the failure of "Christian *tawhidism*." Some work has been done in recent decades that shows specifically the borrowing from medieval Muslim science and learning by non-Muslim European scholars in various disciplines. But no attempt is made in the following chapters to trace, for example, the assimilation of Muslim astronomy in the works and careers of Nicolaus Copernicus, Tycho Brahe, Johannes Kepler, etc., or Western medieval and pre-modern astronomy in general. Instead a few general and specialized works on the borrowing and transmission of Muslim science and learning by Christian Europe or the West are given below for the interested reader.

Islamic Philosophy and History of Astronomy and Technology in General: Selected References

A. Sources of Information

Nasr, Seyyed Hossein. *Islamic Science: An Annotated Bibliography*, 2 vols (Teheran: Imperial Iranian Academy of Philosophy, 1975-78); [Also 3 vols., Lahore: S. M. Ashraf, 1990s].

Sarton, George. *An Introduction to the History of Science*, 3 vols in 5 (Baltimore: Williams & Wilkins Co., 1927-48).

Isis: An International Review Devoted to the History of Science and its Cultural Influences. U.S.A.

MAAS Journal of Islamic Science. The Muslim Association for the Advancement of Science, Aligarh, India.

B. Islamic Astronomy and Related Sciences

Ahmad, Imad-ad-Dean. *Signs in the Heavens: A Muslim Astronomer's Perspective on Religion and Science* (Beltsville, MD: Writers' Inc.-International, 1992).

Bitruji. *Kitab fi al-Haya: On the Principles of Astronomy; an Edition of the Arabic and Hebrew Versions with Translation, Analysis, and an Arabic-Hebrew-English Glossary.* By Bernard R. Goldstein (New Haven: Yale Univ. Press, 1971).

Carmody, Francis J. *Arabic Astronomical and Astrological Sciences in Latin Translation, a Critical Bibliography* (Berkeley: Univ. of California Press, 1956).

From Deferent to Equant: A Volume of Studies in the History of Science in the Ancient and Medieval Near East in Honor of E. S. Kennedy, David A. King and George Saliba, eds. (New York: New York Academy of Sciences, 1987).

Kennedy, Edward S. *A Commentary upon Biruni's Kitab Tahdid al-amakin* (Beirut: American Univ of Beirut, 1973);

—*The Life & Work of Ibn Shatir* (Aleppo: Institute for the History of Arabic Science, Univ of Aleppo, 1976); and

—*Studies in the Islamic Exact Sciences* (Beirut: American Univ of Beirut, 1983).

King, David A. *Islamic Mathematical Astronomy* (London: Variorum Reprints, 1986);

—*Astronomy in the Service of Islam* (Brookfield, Vt, USA: Variorum, 1993); and

—*Nasir al-Din al-Tusi's Memoir on Astronomy. Al-Tadhkira fi Ilm al-Haya.* Commentary by F. J. Ragep (New York: Springer-Verlag, 1993).

Saliba, George. *A History of Arabic Astronomy: Planetary Theories in the Golden Age of Islam* (New York: New York Univ Press, 1994).

Sams o, Julio. *Islamic Astronomy and Medieval Spain* (Brookfield, Vt.: Variorum, 1994).

C. History and Philosophy of Islamic Science, Including Astronomy and Related Sciences: General Works, and Works with Relevant Chapters

Bakar, Osman. *Tawhid and Science: Essays on the History and Philosophy of Islamic Science* (Penang: Secretariat for Islamic Philosophy & Science, Science Univ of Malaysia, 1991).

Al-Biruni Commemorative Volume, ed. Muhammad Said (Karachi: Hamdard Foundation, 1979).

Bucaille, Maurice. *The Bible, the Qur'an, and Science* (Indianapolis: North American Trust Publ., 1978).

Crombie, A.C. *Science, Optics, and Music in Medieval Early Modern Thought* (London: Hambledon, 1990).

The Genius of Arab Civilization: Source of Renaissance, 3rd ed., Hayes, John S., ed. (New York: New York Univ. Press, 1992).

Al-Ghazali. *Tahafut al-Filasafah: Incoherence of the Philosophers*, trans. by Sabih A. Kamali (Toronto: McGill

Univ. Press, 1995).

History of Oriental Astronomy: Proceedings of an International Astronomical Union Colloquium No. 91, New Delhi, India, 13-16 November 1985, G. Swarup, A.K. Bag, K.S. Shukla, eds. (New York: Cambridge Univ Press, 1987).

Al-Hassan, Ahmad Y. and Donald R. Hill. *Islamic Technology : An Illustrated History* (Cambridge: Cambridge Univ. Press, 1986).

Hill, Donald R. *A History of Engineering in Classical and Medieval Times* (La Salle, IL: Open Court Pub. Co., 1984).

A History of Muslim Philosophy, ed. M.M. Sharif, 2 vols (Wiesbaden: Otto Harrassowitz, 1963-66).

Hourani, George F. *Essays on Islamic Philosophy and Science* (Albany: State Univ of New York Press, 1975).

Islam, Philosophy, and Science (Paris: UNESCO Press, 1981).

Nasr, Seyyed H. *An Introduction to Islamic Cosmological Doctrines* (Cambridge: Harvard Univ. Press, 1964);

—*Science and Civilization in Islam* (Cambridge: Harvard Univ. Press, 1968); and

—*Islamic Science: An Illustrated Study* (London: World of Islam Festival, 1976).

Qadir, C.A. *Philosophy and Science in the Islamic World.*

Ibn Rushd, *Tahafut al-Tahafut: The Incoherence of the Incoherence,* trans. S. Van den Bergh, 2 vols. (London, 1969);

—*Kitab Fasl al-Maqal (the Harmony of Religion and*

Philosophy), trans. George F. Hourani (Leiden: E.J. Brill, 1959).

Sayili, Aydin M. *The Observatory in Islam* (Ankara: Turk Tarih Kurumu Basimevi, 1960).

Studies in the Islamic Exact Sciences, David A. King and Mary H. Kennedy, eds. (Beirut: American Univ of Beirut, 1983).

Swerdlow, N.M., and O. Neugabauer. *Mathematical Astronomy in Copernicus's De Revolutionibus* (New York: Springer-Verlag, 1984).

D. Some Primary and Secondary References on Western Borrowing of Islamic Science and Learning in General

Sarton, George. *An Introduction to the History of Science*, 3 vols. in 5; 1:6-17, 503, 521-3, 544, 587, 620, 626, 694, 701, 707-709, 721-23, 563f; 2:1-3, 98f, 109, 113-17, 167-81, 282- 86, 321-30, 338-49, 350-53, 355-61, 485, 491-95, 561-69, 709, 716-24, 808f, 815,818, 829-61, 914-21, 934-44; and 3:67-71, 426-69, 1021, 1071-78, 1373-96; *et passim*.

Ahmad, Imad-ad-Dean. *Signs in the Heavens*, op.cit., esp. Chapter 6, "The impact of Islamic Astronomy on the West."

History of Mankind; Cultural and Scientific Development. Vol. IV: The Foundations of the Modern World, eds., Louis Gottschalk, *et al*, UNESCO, esp. chap. 13, "Science and technology between c. 1300 and c. 1530," (4: 789-828) where the authors, relying exclusively on Western scholarship of Sarton, Thorndike, etc., present views similar to those presented in Husaini, below.

Husaini, S. Waqar Ahmed. *Islamic Environmental Systems Engineering*, pp. 52f, 63-66, 155-61; and *Islamic Science and Public Policies*, pp. 9-15; for a summary of borrowing and assimilation of Islamic science and philosophy in general by the West from about the second century A.H. / eighth century A.D. to tenth century A.H./ sixteenth A.D. century, and its sociological ramifications.

Nasr, Seyyed Hossein. *Science and Civilization in Islam; An Introduction to Islamic Cosmological Doctrines; Islamic Science: An Illustrated Study;* and his other works.

CHAPTER 3

Creation of the Universe: God the Creator

Introduction

This chapter presents verses of the Qur'an on the "origination" of the universe in relation to God as its Originator, Creator, etc. This is compared with man's pre-Qur'anic and modern secular views.

The Qur'an on God as the Originator and Creator of the Universe: Duty to Study Astronomy, Condemnation of Astrologers.

> *See they not how God begins* (yabda'u) *creation, then He repeats it; truly that is easy for God!*
> *Say: Travel through the earth and see how God did begin creation; so will God produce a later creation. For God has power over all things.* (29: 19-20; *cf.* Asad's translation)

> *[Hallowed be] He who has created* (khalaqa) *seven*

heavens in harmony with one another. No fault will you see in the creation of the Most Gracious. And turn your vision once more; can you see any flaw?
Yea, turn your vision again and yet again; your vision will fall back upon you, dazzled and truly defeated. (67:3-4)

And God's is the east and the west; and wherever you turn, there is God's countenance. Behold, God is infinite, all-knowing.
And yet they assert, 'God has taken unto Himself a son!' Limitless is He in His glory! Nay, but His is all that is in the heavens and on earth; all things devoutly obey His will.
The Originator (badi'a) *is He of the heavens and the earth; and when He wills a thing to be, He but says unto it, 'Be', and it is.* (2: 115-117; *also* 6: 100-102)

Even if We had opened to them a gateway to heaven and they had ascended, on and on, up to it, they would surely have said, 'It is only our eyes that are spellbound! Nay, we are people bewitched!'
And, indeed, We have set up in the heavens great constellations, and endowed them with beauty for the beholders (li-nazirin); *and We have made them secure* (hafiznaha) *against every accursed satan, except that anyone who seeks to learn by stealth is pursued by a flame clear to see* (shihab mubin). (15:14-18 n16; *also* 37:7; 41:12; *and* 15:17 Asad n16; 2:14 n10)

Have they, then, not seen how little of the sky and the earth lies open before them, and how much is hidden from them? If we so willed, we could cause the earth to swallow them, or We could cause fragments of the sky to fall down upon them? In this, behold, there is a message [ayah] indeed for every servant [of God] who is accustomed to turn to Him. (34:9)

Summary and Explanation

The root verb *khalaqa*, "He created," and its derivatives occur over 200 times in as many verses in the Qur'an[1]. Some verses use words like beginning, *yabda'u*, the Originator, *fatir*, and the one who started in the first instance, *badi'a*. God as the *Rab* (the Sustainer, Nourisher, Manager, etc.) of the universe occurs in over 950 verses while the word Allah, God, with its derivatives occurs nearly 2700 times! Thus God is never to be denied or ignored as the creator of the heavens and earth in any instance and aspect.

God is the Creator and Manager of His laws of nature. The singular *Ayah* (34:9) and its derivatives are used about 382 times in the Qur'an. *Ayat* means "signs," "messages," "miracles', and "verses" of the Qur'an. *Ayat Allah* (signs of God), mean the phenomena, forces and laws in the physical universe as well as the moral laws and ideological principles embodied in the "verses" of the Qur'an. They are also referred to as God's "determination or ordination" (*taqdir*, 41:12); the tradition , custom, or way (*sunnah*) of God; the human nature or true natural disposition (*fitrah*) created by God; the creation (*khalq*) of God, etc. The secularists and atheists refer to them as merely "nature," "the laws of nature," etc.

Many questions can be asked based only on the verses quoted above. What are the means and methods man should undertake to physically see, make observations, experience and undertake experiments in astronomical studies? What are the roles of sight, observation, travel on the earth and in space, and other means of induction and deduction in learning about the origination, creation, and development of the universe? How can man judge that there are no defects in the creation and functioning of the universe? And what are the capabilities and limitations of human knowledge? What are the fragments from the sky falling upon the earth? Are these the meteoroids (pieces of iron and rock) entering the earth's atmosphere, burning up in the atmosphere as meteors, and others falling upon earth's surface as meteorites? Is the "flame" surrounding the bodies in space a reference to their heat and radiation? And is the warning against approaching them "stealthily" a reference to the prerequisites for successful space travel by the explorers who want to "see" and learn about the beauty of the universe? What is meant by the beginning and end of the universe? What was there before the heavens and the earth were created? What is that "smoke" that existed before the heavenly bodies were created, and when they are made to end by God? Are astronomers and other scientists the observers of the heavenly bodies? And what does it take to make them the servants of God who appreciate the beauty and perfection in the universe created by God? Who are those people who can be overwhelmed with evidence on perfection in the physical universe, yet refuse to acknowledge God and implement His moral order and purpose?

The purpose and goal of the Islamic scientific method, applied to astronomy and cosmology also, is to recognize God as the Originator and Creator of everything on the earth and in the heavens, learn about His laws in nature and human activities, and apply them according to God's moral commands.

The universe is not self-created or self-subsisting. By issuing a command to "be," God brings into existence any "original" or first creation. He creates and recreates things through operation of His laws of their being. The heavens and the earth did not exist as they are now; they were a kind of "smoke" (41:11). When God brings in the Day of Judgment, ending our universe or the solar system, He will turn them again into "smoke"(44:10).

There is orderliness, regularity, punctuality and predictability, and no arbitrariness and capricious changes in the universe. There is wisdom and intelligence, beauty and perfection, utility and moral purpose in every thing that God has created. Such is the case with the movements of the sun and the moon as well as the fall of great nations who break God's laws of social dynamics. ... *Thus: no change will you find in the* (sunnah) *tradition of God. Indeed, no deviation will you find in the sunnah of God.* (35:43).

Thus the study of astronomical sciences by rational means should lead men to affirm the existence and oneness of God and His attributes. God has determined (*qaddara*) the laws of being and functions of stars and planets too;

they have no power over man, and are inferior and subservient to man. These are principles of Islamic monotheism or *tawhid:* "oneness, unity, and integration." *Tawhid* is incompatible with secularism inasmuch as it ignores God as the Creator and Sustainer of the universe. Thus no science or knowledge should be pursued under secularism; in fact, it is blasphemy: contempt or indignity offered to God by denying Him, and His jurisdiction over His own creation.

The Qur'an, thus, provides the basic philosophical principles of Islamic astronomy and cosmology. It is an Islamic duty *(fard)* of man to seek even the more difficult cosmological knowledge about origination and creation of the universe. However, he should realize that rational knowledge is subject to the limitations of time, space, relativity of human thought, etc. There is so much outside man's human powers in God's heavens and earth that he does not and will never know. Man should not try to "steal" knowledge; he should not try to know the unknowable by resorting to wrong or false means through the occult and esoteric sciences, or pseudo-sciences like astrology.

When he enters the heavens or space, man will face "a seeable, conspicuous or knowable flame" (*shihab mubin*, 15:14-18). The stars (*kawakib*) and constellations (*buruj*) are surrounded, or protected by God (*hafiznaha*), by a flame. Inspite of that, space exploration is open "for those who look at it, or undertake intellectual investigation, to gain knowledge" (*li-nazirin*, 15:16); but this must be done with the right methods and motives, and for proper uses. Other verses of the Qur'an give the moral and utilitarian functions of the heavenly bodies. These are obtaining light and energy, locating direction, keeping an account of and predicting time, etc. Astronomical studies should lead to belief in God, and application of His ethical determinations given in the Qur'an in the conduct of our lives, society and civilization. Astronomy should not be used to develop astrology. Astrologers are accursed and rebellious satans (67:5, nn 5, 6;37:6-11, n 6) because the method, content, and purpose of their knowledge are false, wrong and deceitful. They are guilty of the worst kind of corruption and leading mankind astray; they do so by corruption of the rational and moral foundations of knowledge.

Pre-Qur'anic Astronomical and Cosmological Sciences, and the Qur'an

Before the Qur'an was revealed, during the first century B.H./sixth century A.D., the geo-centric theory was most influential through the *Almagest* of Ptolemy (second century A.D.). He was the Alexandrian astronomer who had developed the ideas of Hipparchus (second century B.C.), and Eudoxus and Aristotle (fourth century B.C.). This theory taught that the planets, the sun and moon, and the stars revolve around the earth. The early Muslims had the *Almagest* translated into Arabic. They opposed this earth-centered theory, reformed the Ptolemaic model, and introduced the heliocentric view of the universe in which the planets revolve around the sun. This Muslim model was borrowed by the Polish scientist, Copernicus, who became a student of Islamic astronomy when he moved to Italy. Much of Southern and Western Europe had been adopting and assimilating Muslim sciences and philosophy for several centuries directly through Arabic works, and through their translations into Latin and other European languages. The West celebrates this medieval Islamic model as "the beginnings of modern astronomy," but as "the Copernican Revolution." This "first modern breakthrough in understanding the universe" is attributed to the publication in A.D.1543 of *Concerning the Revolutions of the Celestial Spheres* by Copernicus.

Hindu-Buddhist India was at the frontiers of knowledge, including astronomy mixed with astrology, during first century B.H./sixth century A.D. . The most influential names of these times were Aryabhata I (b. A.D. 476), Latadeva, and Varahamihira (d. A.D. 587). Varahamihira wrote a treatise on mathematics and astronomy which combined Hindu trigonometry and astrology with Greek knowledge. It is celebrated as one of the outstanding "scientific" works of the time; but Varahamihira's *Brhajjataka* became the basic Hindu reference on horoscopes in South Asia.

The most important points to note here are, first, that the scientific worldview presented in the Qura'n in the first century A.H./seventh century A.D., concerning the universe and cosmology, was in basic disagreement with the most influential and accepted viewpoints dominating then in Europe, North Africa, West Asia and South Asia. The latter represented Greek, Roman, Alexandrian, Syriac, Sassanian or Persian, Hindu, Buddhist, and Chinese science and civilization. How did Muhammad, an illiterate man of the Arabian peninsula, know the ideas presented in the

Qur'an? The Qur'anic "guidance" on the astronomical and cosmological sciences was to be discovered and confirmed gradually in recent centuries, particularly in recent decades. Secondly, as regards the philosophic and religious points of view, the Greek, Hindu and other religions were dominated by polytheism, nature worship, mythology, etc. Their gods, goddesses, and demons invoked conflicting powers concerning the heavenly bodies and the forces of nature. Judaism and Christianity had lost their monotheism and were in the Dark Ages in relation to science and learning. The linkage of the unique monotheism of Islam, the holistic concept of *tawhid*, with the running of the worlds and managing all the forces and laws of nature, was a unique feature of the Qur'an.

Contemporary Astronomical Sciences and Theories

The Qur'an provides principles of the Islamic philosophy of science and some basic facts. Ours is an orderly universe run by God's laws which are knowable and predictable within the limits of man. Human knowledge on certain subjects in astronomy and cosmology will always take the form of "theories" and "scientific conjectures" rather than observable facts and provable certainties. The universe is too vast and complex to be fully known by man.

The concepts of the "signs" (*ayat*) and "tradition" (*sunnah*) of God as "laws of nature," etc., are consistent with the modern worldview of "secular" science and its scientific method. The defects of secularism as compared with *tawhid* have been pointed out above; the latter is "oneness" or holism that integrates the concept of God the

69

Creator with the creation.

Modern science believes that the universe was created in time, and will end in the course of time. The universe is not eternal and timeless in the past and the future; it had a beginning and it will have an end. For example, astronomical studies have led scientists to believe that the universe contains spots of extreme density and temperature at the core of stars, and areas of low density and temperature such as interstellar matter. This diversity suggests that the universe is not eternal but was created. The logic here is that if the universe was eternal then it would have had equal density and temperature due to thermal and pressure equilibrium. The existence of radioactive materials such as radium and uranium is also a proof that the universe is created since radioactive materials have been found to decay at a regular rate from the time they are formed.

Astronomers believe that the universe started between 10 and 20 billion years ago with an enormous explosion called "the Big Bang." All the matter in the universe was squeezed into a small spot before then; the big bang sent it flying in all directions. According to this theory, the universe has been expanding since the instant it began. At first it consisted chiefly of radiation; most of it has changed into matter in the process of expansion. Since almost all galaxies (a system of stars, dust, and gas held together by gravity) are moving away from each other at very high speeds, there must have been a beginning for the expansion of the universe and, therefore, for the universe itself. Most research seems to indicate that the universe will continue to expand "forever"; but some studies suggest that it may ultimately stop expanding and begin to contract. This may be interpreted as the birth, life and death of the universe.

Another specific example may be given from the scientists' views on the birth and death of stars. Stars, including our sun, are born of vast clouds of gas and dust called the nebulae. Parts of the nebulae begin to contract; they become denser until the temperature at the center becomes so high that thermonuclear reactions are started. Their hydrogen becomes helium, giving out light and enery; thus a star is born. When the stars exhaust their hydrogen, they will die. The sun, and the rest of the objects in the solar system, are estimated to be 4.6 billion years old, and the sun might burn up its hydrogen fuel and stop shining in another 5 billion years.

Conclusion

The above and other ideas are based on cosmological "theories," or scientific predictions about the behaviour of the universe. More specifically, scientists acknowledge that the dates and numbers given concerning far off stars are mere estimates based on "theories." Therefore, we should maintain doubt and uncertainty in cosmological theories, be conscious of the relativity and fallibility of human thought, and accept the Qur'anic admonition above (34: 9): what we know about the heavens and the earth is like what is in or between our hands; and what we do not and cannot know is like all that is out side the palms of our hands, and what is behind us or beyond our backs.

Notes

[1] The verses on God "starting in the first instance," *(yabda'u)*, the creation of the heavens and earth, etc., include: 10:4, 34; 12:76; 21:101-104; 27:64; 29:19-20; 30:11,27; 32:7; and 85:13. The only two verses which refer to God as the Beginner *(badi'a)* of the heavens and earth are 2:117 and 6:101. Verses on God as the Originator *(Fatir)* of the universe are: 6:14, 79; 12:101; 14:10; 30:30 and n. 27; 35:1; 39:46; and 42:11.

[2] *References:* S.v., "Astronomy", "Copernicus", "Cosmology", "Sun", "Ptolemy", "Stars", "Universe", *The World Book Encyclopedia,* 1981. Husaini, *Islamic Science and Public Policies.*

1. Coma Cluster of Galaxies

[Hallowed be] He who has created seven (many) heavens in harmony; no fault will you see in the creation of the Most Gracious. And turn your vision once more; can you see any flaw? Yea, turn your vision again and again; your vision will fall back upon you, dazzled and defeated. **(Qur'an 67:3-4)**

Modern astronomers define a galaxy as an assembly of gas, dust, and millions or billions of stars; a cluster may have thousands of galaxies. Our solar system is a part of the Milky Way Galaxy which is just one of 40 galaxies in a cluster. How big is the universe, or heavens, *samawat?* This image shows hundreds of galaxies in an area of the sky or *sama'* that is visible through the eye on a U.S. coin held at arm's length! The Coma Cluster, 300 million light years from the earth, is estimated to have 1,000 large and thousands of smaller galaxies. Galaxy aNGC 4881, the brightest in the picture, is 300,000 light years in diameter. *"Glorified be the Sustainer of the heavens and the earth, the Sustainer of the Throne, from that which they ascribe (unto Him)."* **(Qur'an 43:82)**

2. Cartwheel Galaxy

It is He who grants life and death; and when He wills a thing to be, He says unto it, 'Be' - and it is. **(Qur'an 40:68)**

Galaxies travel at about two million miles/hour. God made perhaps one of the smaller galaxies intrude into the core of this Galaxy 200 million years ago. This collision created a wave of energy that sent gas and dust in front at 200,000 miles/hour. The wave heated and compressed the Galaxy's dust and gas, and produced the bright blue expanding ring around it which reveals the birth of several billion new stars. This Galaxy is 150,000 light years across in size, and 500 million light years from the earth.

3. The Solar System

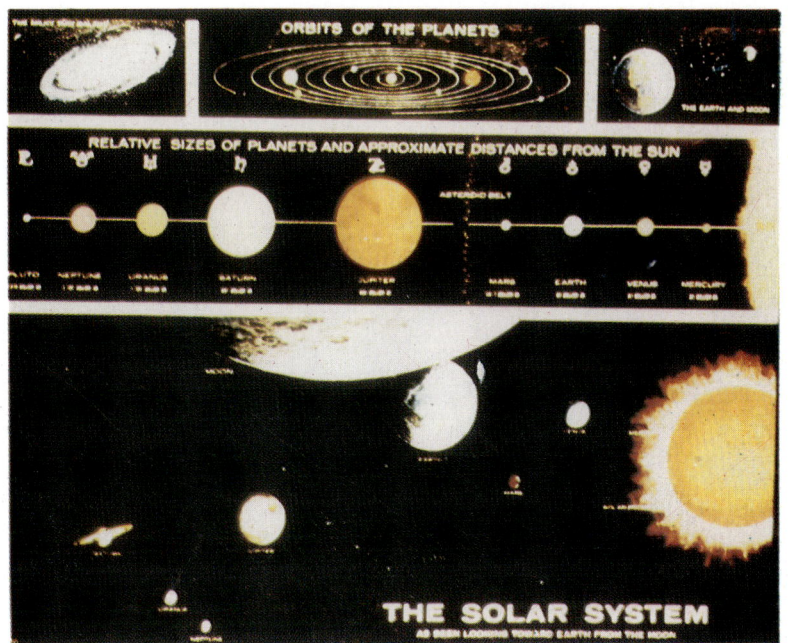

Hallowed is He who has set up in the sky a collection of heavenly bodies, and has placed among them a lamp [the Sun] *and a light-giving moon.* **(Qur'an 25:61)**

Scientists believe that our solar system is one of the billions of members of the Milky Way Galaxy (top left). It comprises a single star (the Sun), nine planets with numerous moons, and a belt of asteroids (minor planets). The image shows the relative sizes of the planets and their position relative to the Sun, the farthest to nearest being Pluto, Neptune, Uranus, Saturn, Jupiter, Mars, Earth, Venus, and Mercury. The asteroid belt is between Jupiter and Mars.

4. Gaseous Ring Around Supernova 1987A

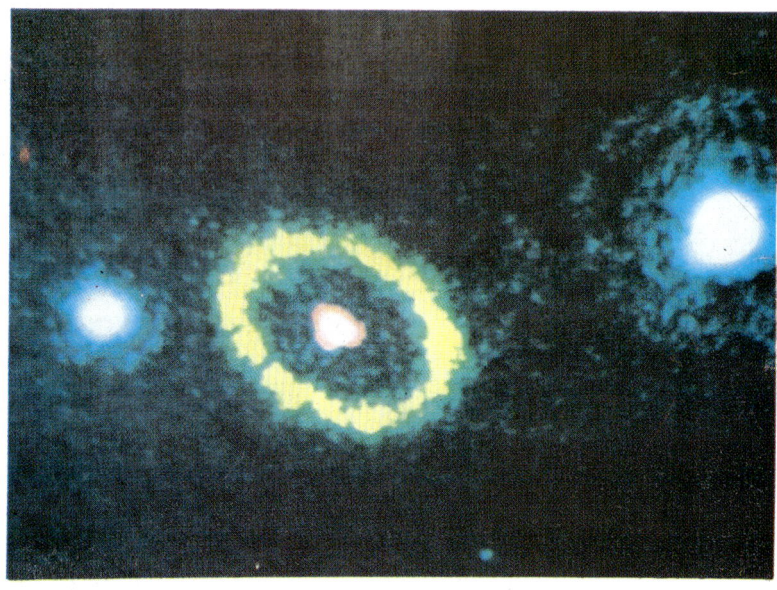

Have they, then, not observed that God, who has created the heavens and the earth and never been wearied by their creation, has the power to bring the dead back to life? Yea, He has the power to will anything. **(Qur'an 46:33)**

Supernovas are massive old dying stars which burn up most of their remaining helium in giant explosions. Supernova 1987A exploded in 1987. This image shows an elliptical ring of gas, about 1.4 light years across, surrounding the expanding debris from the explosion. The gaseous ring will eventually disintegrate as this debris collides with it. The Hubble Space Telescope is providing data that scientists will use to theorize on the evolution of stars and their death.

CHAPTER 4

The Universe:
Astrologers vs Astronomy

Introduction

Shaytan, satan, denotes in the Qur'an a force, impulse, person, etc., that is "remote from or opposed to" (*shatana*) what is true and good, esp. God and His laws and ethical postulates.

Rujum, (*rajam*, sing.) means "throwing [something] like a stone" at random; metaphorically, it means "making (something) the object of guesswork," or "speaking conjecturally."

The Qur'an on Astrologers vs Astronomy

And, indeed, We have set up in the heavens great constellations (buruj, stars), *and endowed them with beauty for the beholders* (li-nazirin); *and We have made them secure* (hafiznaha) *against every accursed satan* (shaytan), *except that anyone who seeks to learn by stealth is pursued by a flame clear to see* (shihab mubin)." (15:16-18, Asad nn15-17).

And, indeed, We have adorned the skies nearest to the earth with lamps [stars], *and have made them the object of futile guesses* (rujum) *for the satans* [the evil men, i.e., astrologers]; *and for them have We readied suffering through a blazing flame.*
And suffering in hell awaits all who reject (kafaru) *their Sustainer; and how vile a journey's end.*(67: 5-6, Asad nn5, 6)

Verily, your God is One, the Sustainer of the heavens and the earth and all that is between them, and the Sustainer of all the points of sunrise!
Behold, We have adorned the skies nearest to the earth with the beauty of the stars (al-kawakib).
and have made them secure (hifza) *against every rebellious satan* (shaytan),
[so that] *they should not be able to hear the host on high, but shall be repelled from all sides, cast out, with lasting suffering in store for them; except that anyone who does succeed in snatching a glimpse* [of such knowledge], *he is pursued by a piercing flame.*
And now ask them to enlighten thee: Were they more difficult to create than all those [marvels] *that We have created? For, behold, them have We created out of clay commingled with water!"* (37:4-11, Asad n6)

Summary and Explanation

The sun, moon, other stars and planets, the earth and all that is on it, have all been created by God for man and to be of service (*saqqara*) to him[1]. God has made them subservient to His laws, and to man by His command[2]; they obediently pursue their courses[3]. Their legitimate functions and uses are to give light and energy, guidance in travel, to be a source of reckoning for many purposes, etc.[4] It is even possible to approach them; but those who do so will find that these heavenly bodies are surrounded by a "flame" that is "piercing" and "very apparent."

The heavenly bodies should not be used to "steal" knowledge; that is, to influence and predict the future through astrology. This is wrong and illegitimate according to Islamic ethics. The astrologers are satans, or extremely bad people. They are rebellious against the fundamental principles of Islamic ethics. Man has been endowed with moral freedom and responsibility; he is not determined by the movements of stars and the other assumptions of astrology. He has the capacity to make the universe serve him; and he has the duty to do so according to the principles given in the Qur'an. The astrologers are not applying true knowledge; they are indulging in mere wild guesses and harming those who become victims of their elaborate lies and deceptions. Therefore, they are satans; they are the worst kind of people because they have debased the very concept of knowledge based on the truth of facts and laws of nature as created and determined by God. They have made falsehood and deception a profession. Thus astrology, that deals with the horoscopes of individuals and also predictions of the future of events and institutions, is condemned in the Qur'an in the strongest possible terms. The astrologers are satan.

The heavenly bodies are themselves "protected" from the powers attributed to them of knowing and determining the future. They are merely creations of God and "obedient" to Him; they are totally subject to God's laws of the physical sciences and astronomy. Unlike man, they have no moral freedom.

Only God determines the future according to His laws that govern nature, man and society. However, there are people who can also know, determine and predict the future within the limitations of man set by God. Their description and characteristics are given in the Qur'an. They are the people of knowledge (*'ulama*, scholars, scientists)[5], and they are those who have acquired knowledge (*'ulu al-'ilm*)[6], and they are those who are soundly and sincerely rooted in true knowledge (*rasiqun fi al-'ilm*).[7] They can make predictions based on their knowledge and wisdom concerning the "signs" or laws of God. Thus God's moral and physical laws, and their application by qualified men, determine the destiny of individuals and nations; these are not determined by stars.

Pre-Qur'anic Views about Astrology and Astronomy[8]

According to astrology, the heavenly bodies influence what happens on earth; they form patterns which can reveal a person's character, and the future of persons and events. Astrology began probably before 2000 B.C. in Babylonia (modern Iraq). People believed that the five planets they knew then sent out forces which had characteristics. One of the planets which seemed red to them (Mars) was linked with anger, aggression, and war.

Astrologers draw a circular chart called the horoscope or birth chart. Most often it shows the position of the earth and stars at the time of a person's birth. The four elements of the horoscope are the earth, the planets, the "zodiac," and the "houses." They make no distinction between a star and planets. They put the earth at the center of the solar system, and believe that the positions of the planets in relation to the earth reveal a person's character and future. The zodiac, a group of stars which seem to encircle the earth, are divided into 12 equal parts called the signs; they believe that the signs of the zodiac determine how the planets affect a person's character. The earth's surface is divided into 12 parts too; these, called houses, are supposed to represent characteristics of a person's life. The zodiac was probably developed in ancient Egypt; the Babylonians adopted it after 1000 B.C. Astrologers developed the system of casting horoscopes between 600-200 B.C.

The ancient Greeks and Romans also practiced astrology and strongly influenced its development. Varahamihira (d. 587 A.D.) of India was one of the most original and influential scientists of his century. His scientific works combined Hindu trigonometry and astrology with Greek knowledge; but they were permeated with astrology. Varahamihira's *Brhajjataka* became the basic work in Hindu judicial astrology (dealing with horoscopes of persons) and genethliac astrology (dealing with the future of events and institutions). Thus there was no distinction between astronomy as we now know it and astrology before the Qur'an was revealed in early first century A.H./seventh A.D. century. They were thoroughly mixed together. Astrology dominated the principles and uses of astronomy.

Contemporary Relations between Astrology and Astronomy

Modern science has disproved the basic principles of astrology. The earth is not the center of the solar system. The position of the earth in space has changed since ancient times; hence the signs of the zodiac do not match the constellations after which they were named. There is no scientific basis for astrology.

Conclusions

In refuting the scientific bases of astrology, modern science has confirmed the Qur'anic critique of astrology. In this modern science has followed the Islamic methods, purposes, and uses of the heavenly bodies in the development and application of astronomy. It is said, however, that the interest in astrology and its use is stronger now and in modern times than ever before in the world. It was only in the Qur'an that the strongest attacks were made against astrology on two counts. First, astrology was refuted on epistemological grounds; it is not knowledge at all but a human invention through mere wild guesswork. The Qur'anic views about the universe created and operated by God's physical laws, the methods of knowing them, and the rational and ethical pursuit and evaluation of knowledge, were all opposed to astrology; they led man towards astronomy in the context of Islamic monotheism, or *tawhid*. Secondly, the astrologers were attacked as satans; namely people whose beliefs, motives, objectives, and sincerity are purposely wrong and willfully distorted. Astrology was identified with *kufr:* the denial and rejection of God, and the integrated Qur'anic rational and ethical systems.

Notes

1   Qur'an 14:33; 16:12; 29:61; 31:29; 35:13; and 39:5.

2   *Ibid.,* 7:54; 16:12;

3   *Ibid.,* 14:33.

4   *Ibid.,* 6:96f, n81; 55:5.

5   *Ibid.,* 35:28; cf. 26:197.

6   *Ibid.,* 3:18; 16:27; 17:107; 22:54; 28:80; 29:49; 30:56; 34:6; 47:16; and 58:11.

7   *Ibid.,* 3:7, nn5, 7; 4:162.

8   *S.v.* "Astrology," *World Book Encyclopedia, 1981.* On Hindu astrology, Husaini, *Islamic Science and Public Policies,* p. 5. For "Islamic" critiques of astrology and other pseudo-sciences like alchemy by the early scholars who developed the Islamic theory of knowledge and its classifications, see the references in , "An Introduction to Islamic and Comparative Astronomy ..." and also works of classical scholars like al-Ghazali (d. AH 505/1111 AD) and Ibn Khaldun (d. AH 808/1406 AD): Al-Ghazali, *Book of Knowledge,* trans. of *Kitab al-'Ilm* of Al-Ghazali's *Ihya' 'Ulum al-Din* by N. A. Faris (Lahore: S.M. Ashraf, 1966); Al-Ghazali, *The Faith and Practice of al-Ghazali (Al-Munqidh min al-Dalal* trans, W.M. Watt (London: George Allen & Unwin Ltd., 1953): Ibn Khaldun, *The Muqaddimah: An Introduction to History,* trans. Franz Rosenthal, (Princeton: Princeton Univ Press., 1967); Muhsin Mahdi, *Ibn Khaldun's Philosophy of History* (London: George Allen & Unwin, 1957); these are summarized in Husaini, *Islamic Environmental Systems Engineering,* chap. 3.

CHAPTER 5

The Universe: Structure and Stages of Development

Introduction

This chapter explains a few key words, and the structure of "the heavens and the earth" and stages in their development. The "seven" or several heavens could refer to our solar system.

Sama' is "something that is above [another thing]." *Al-sama'* means the sky, and *al-samawat*, the skies or heavens. These words could connote the cosmic space, a part of the heavens comprising our solar system or even the galaxies, etc., since they are all above the earth. Such literal Qur'anic Arabic terms should be also understood technically in the context of the knowledge of the times within certain criteria.

A "day," *yawm*, also denotes in Arabic extremely long periods of time. This is also explicit in the Qur'an: "... in your Sustainer's sight a day is like a thousand years of your reckoning" (22:47; cf. 32:5), and "... a day the length whereof is fifty thousand years" (70:4). Thus "days" in reference to astronomy, geology, and the Hereafter may mean ages, eons, or very long periods.

"Seven" (*Sab'a*) in Arabic usage also means "several." Thus the "seven" heavens would mean several units or parts of space, the universe, or solar system; the "seven paths," *sab'a tarai'q*, may mean several celestial orbits; and the "seven firm ones," *sab'a shidada*, might refer to several cosmic systems "built over you" by God. Similarly the "seven *tibaq*" may refer to several heavenly bodies that are "placed one above another," that "are in harmony with one another," or are in "one state or stage or another."

The Qur'an on the Structure of the "Seven Heavens"

What is amiss with you that you cannot look forward to God's majesty,
seeing that He has created you in successive stages?
Do you not see how God has created seven heavens in full harmony with one another (tibaq),
and has set up within them the moon as a light, and set up the sun as a lamp? (71: 13-16, Asad n8; also 67:3-4, n2)

And, indeed, We have created above you seven paths [celestial orbits, *sab'a tarayiq*]; *and never are We unmindful of creation."* (23:17, n7; cf. 78:6, 12-13, n7)

God is He who has created seven heavens and, like them, of the earth. Through all of them flows down from on high, unceasingly, the command (amr), *so that you might come to know that God has the power to will anything, and that God encompasses all things with His knowledge.* (65: 12, n19)

The Qur'an on Development of "the Heavens, the Earth, and What is Between them" in "Six Days"

It is God who has created the heavens and the earth and all that is between them in six days, and He is established on the throne [of His almightiness]. *²You have none to protect you from God, and none to intercede for you: will you not, then, bethink yourselves? He governs all that exists* [or He directs the ordinance, amr] *from the skies to the earth; and in the end all shall ascend unto Him on a Day the length whereof will be* [like] *a thousand years of your reckoning.* (32:3-4, Asad n4; see also 7:54, n43; 11:7, nn10, 11; 25:59; 50:38)

Say: Would you indeed deny Him who has created the earth in two days [ayyam, eons]? *And do you give associates to Him, the Sustainer of the worlds (al-'alamin)?*

For He placed firm mountains on it [the earth], *towering above its surface, and bestowed blessings on it, and equitably apportioned its means of subsistence to all who would seek it:* [and all this He created] *in four days* [eons].

And He applied His design to the skies which were smoke (dukhan); *and He said to them and the earth,*

'Come, both of you, willingly or unwillingly!' They
both responded, 'We do come in obedience'.
And He decreed that they become seven heavens in two
days [eons], *and imparted to each heaven its command*
(amr). *And He adorned the skies nearest to the earth*
with lights [stars] *and made them secure. Such is* the
determination (taqdir) *of the Almighty , the All-*
knowing. (41: 9-12, Asad nn7, 12, 13. cf. 2:29, n20;
7:54, n43; 29:20, n20)

Summary and Explanation

What scientific meaning may be given in the light of
contemporary knowledge to the Qur'anic Arabic words for
skies or heavens (*samawat*), days (*ayyam*), the worlds (*al-*
'alamin), etc. Is the solar system, or the whole universe, or
both, meant by the phrase, "the heavens, the earth and
what is between them"? Does the phrase, "the seven
heavens," limit the "several" heavens to a few, such as our
solar system? How should we exercise the Qur'anic duty
"to see, observe, investigate, and study," (*taraw*) as applied
to creation of the heavens and the earth in view of the
limitations of human knowledge? What is the probability
of man knowing when and how the solar system, and the
sun and earth and moon individually, were born and
developed when this took place long ago over lengthy
periods? What are the *tibaq* or stages in the creation of the
earth, in its development until it became capable of
supporting life , and in the creation of our solar system,
each of which took two "days"? What is the meaning of the
"skies nearest to the earth" which are adorned with
"lights" (stars, *kawakib*)? What, then, are the skies or

heavens farther and farther away from the earth?

If there are "seven" or several heavens, "and, like them, of the earth," is it an allusion to other planets and their moons within our solar system? Or is that also a reference to other earths with similar environmental conditions and living creatures in other heavenly systems? What is the significance, in this context, to repeated mention of the worlds (al-'alamin), and Muhammad being a blessing for the worlds? Man is required to use his senses and logic, avoid mere wishful thinking and conjecture, and offer evidence or proof for his assertions (22:52; 53:24; and 2:111; 21:24; 27:64; 28:75). How do we apply the criteria of this Islamic scientific method in astronomical studies when these produce theories based on non-verifiable assumptions and extrapolations?

The "seven" or several heavens are probably the solar system, and not the whole universe. The verse 71:16 above makes it explicit that God placed the sun and the moon "within" (fi-hinna) the "seven heavens created in harmony with one another (tibaq)." Several verses also make it clear that the "seven heavens" are different from the earth because they are mentioned separately.

God created the earth in "two days." In another "two days" He endowed the earth with its geophysical features like mountains, and developed His "provisions or blessings" on earth so that it became capable of providing sustenance to all kinds of life. The heavens were once a "smoke"; in another "two days," He created out of it "seven heavens," including the light-giving stars in the heavens nearest to the earth; these several heavens are, perhaps, our solar system. There are seven verses in which the creation of "the heavens and earth" in "six days" is mentioned; three of these verses also add "and what is between them." This may refer again to our solar system rather than "the whole universe" as defined elsewhere. God created (*khalaqa*) this solar system in "days" whose time scale is different from our earth-days. This process took place in stages (*tibaq*), over long geologic and astronomical ages, or eons. We may call it the evolution of our solar system and the earth.

God imparted to each heaven its command (*amr*), or the laws for its existence and His governance. The sun, moon, earth, "each heavenly body" and the whole universe, are all obedient to God's determination (*taqdir*) for them. We need to learn and know these *amr* and *taqdir*; this means, in secular terminology, that we must try to know the laws of nature concerning the astronomical phenomena. There is a most important "scientific" justification for the denunciation in the Qur'an of *shirk*: association of beings or powers with God. There cannot be rival sources for physical or moral laws. If there was a god for each of the few stars and planets in our solar system, there will be chaos due to conflicting wills and laws. A universe under such a system is impossible to be created or governed. Thus knowledge of the structure, development, and governance of the universe should lead men to affirmation in *tawhid*: the Oneness of God; and the integration of His laws concerning the sciences and ethics so that application of science and technology is not divorced from morality. Thus *tawhid* requires that decisions in science policy be made under Islamic morality rather than due to realpolitique, pragmatism, utilitarianism, situational ethics, etc.

Pre-Qur'anic Views on the Structure and Development of the Earth, Moon, and Sun

What were the ideas prevailing in different world cultures at the beginning of the first century A.H./seventh century A.D.? The Qur'an was revealed at this time to an illiterate person, Muhammad, in a most backward region of the times, Arabia. Astronomy had been developed, unlike in Arabia, in many civilizations by the first century A.H./ seventh century A.D.. These included the Chinese, Hindu, Babylonian, Egyptian, Greek, Maya, Aztec and others. Some of these had even developed some mathematical astronomy. However, this early astronomy was dominated by two traditions. First, mythology explained many issues in astronomy and cosmology through "creative myths." They associated the origin of the world, the functions of the heavenly bodies, and geophysical features and forces of the earth, with gods, goddesses, heroes, spirits, etc. For example, the sky god was Zeus in Greek, and Indra in Hindu mythology; this warrior god ruled the sky. This common feature is explained by the fact that a people had flourished in the area east of the Volga river, Russia, several thousand years earlier; one group of these Indo-Europeans migrated westward and settled in Greece, and the other settled in ancient India as the Aryans. Secondly, the tradition of astrology did not invoke the power and laws of God to give man the power to learn, control and use natural phenomena beneficially; rather it bestowed power upon the stars to decide the destiny of man and societies. At that time the Jews and Christians of Europe, who are basically monotheistic, were living in the Dark Ages. Islamic learning and culture began to impact upon them at least from the second century A.H./eighth century A.D. Thus the ideas associated above with the Qur'anic verses were unknown in the religious or rational learning and practice of these civilizations. The development of "scientific" astronomy had to await the revelation and application of the Qur'an. The Islamic intellectual tradition started the long battle to divorce astronomy from mythology and astrology.

Contemporary Theories on the Structure and Evolution of the Solar System.

What is the relation between the Qur'anic ideas and contemporary astronomical facts and theories?

Man did start looking at the sky "scientifically" with his naked eyes. Then he began using mathematical sciences, astronomical instruments, and observatories. This kind of advancement was made first in the medieval Muslim cultures, including Muslim Spain and Southern Europe. In recent decades man has been using more powerful telescopes and also spectroscopes, computers, radio astronomy, etc. Manned and unmanned space explorations have been undertaken since 1957. The Milky Way galaxy is visible from anywhere on the earth. The Andromeda Nebula galaxy, more than two million light-years away, is visible only from the Northern Hemisphere. The Small and Large Megallenic Clouds, two other galaxies about 200,000 light-years away, are visible from only the Southern Hemisphere. Thus our eyes can see four galaxies from the earth. Astronomers believe there may be billions of them.

The structure and size of the universe, and the distances involved, may be imagined by a few examples. A light-year is about 9.46 trillion kilometers (10^{13} km). The orbit of the moon around the earth would fit inside a cube whose length, breadth, and depth are each one million (10^6) km. The entire solar system will fill a tiny part of a cube of 10^{12} km, or one-tenth light-year side; the rest would be empty space. This shows how far away is even the nearest star from the sun. A cube of 10^{18} km side will be about 100,000 light-years per side; this region will enclose the Milky Way galaxy. Our solar system is about 30,000 light-years from the center of this galaxy. A region which is 100 million light-years on each side would contain thousands of galaxies; but scientists claim they have photographed millions of galaxies through telescopes! Thus the "paths" (*tarayiq*), or the orbits and regions, of the galaxies and their individual stars are in harmonious relations with each other inspite of their vast numbers. They are "above one another" held together in their own clusters by their gravities; they do not stray away from their orbits, colliding with each other, and creating havoc in the heavens. There is *tibaq*, harmony, in the universe.

Since the 1950s scientists believe they are getting closer to learning how and when the solar system was formed. They believe that the Milky Way was formed about 10 to 15 billion years ago. Some "monistic theories" suggest that all parts of the solar system were formed from a single cloud of gas at the same time; this is perhaps the "smoke," *dukhan,* mentioned in the Qur'an (41:11). Scientists have studied radioactivity of meteorites falling upon the earth, of moon rock and soil brought by astronauts, etc. They believe, based on this evidence, that our solar system was formed about 4.6 billion years ago.

Scientists have a better knowledge of the moon now due to the recent space travels, moon explorations, and related scientific studies. The moon, early in its history, may have been only about 10,000 miles from the earth. The moon's orbit is becoming larger as the earth's spinning has been slowing down. Craters are the most numerous features of the moon's surface; they were formed between 3.9 to 4.6 billion years ago. The largest and oldest may have been created when planetesimals (masses of gas congealed into solid objects) landed on and formed the moon itself. Other large craters were probably formed when large solid bodies from space (comets, asteroids, etc.) struck the moon. Billions of small craters have been found on the moon by the bombardment of meteoroids (pieces of iron and stone). Most of the rocky lowlands, called maria, were formed between 3.3 to 3.8 billion years ago; this was due to great flows of lava (molten rock) that cooled on the moon's surface. Thus the moon has been undergoing changes during its life of a few "days."

Scientists know as little about the earth's earliest stages as they do about the birth of the solar system. Measurements of radioactivity in rocks have led scientists to believe that the oldest rocks ever discovered are almost 3½ billion years old. They suppose that the earth began as a mass of rock, without water, surrounded by a cloud of gas. Radioactivity and pressure produced the heat to melt the earth's interior. The heavy materials like iron sank while the silicate rocks, rich in oxygen, rose to the surface forming the earth's crust. Heating of the earth's interior may have caused other chemicals to rise too, forming water and the atmospheric gases. The water thus created collected over the ages in the low places of the crust to form the oceans. As land developed, precipitation and rivers carried the dissolved salts from weathering rocks to make the oceans salty. The earth's earliest atmosphere probably did not contain much oxygen. As the earth aged, oxygen, freed from the rocks and soil, must have escaped into the atmosphere. Thus an environment developed that was favourable for the "evolution" of plants and animals.

Scientists believe the earth once formed a single land mass, Pangaea, and a single ocean, the Panthalassa. About 200 million years ago Pangaea began to break apart into two land masses. The present day continents were formed gradually over millions of years through drifting of the land masses. The plate tectonics theory tries to explain the continental drift; the motion of these rigid plates, overlying the molten rock mantle under them, also explains the formation of mountains and deep ocean beds, and the occurrence of earthquakes and volcanoes. This theory states that the plates move ½ to 4 inches per year.

The history of the earth is revealed to geologists through the study of rock formations; and the study of fossils, like a piece of an animal's body, provides evidence to paleontologists to develop their theories about the history of life on earth. Thus the earth is divided into six "eras"; the Azoic, Archeozoic and Preterozoic eras cover almost the first 4 billion years of earth's life. The Paleozoic era is divided into seven "periods" lasting from the last 600 million to 225 million years. The fifth, Mesozoic Era, with three periods, lasted from 225 million to 65 million years ago. We now live in the Cenozoic Era, divided into two periods and six "epochs," covering the last 65 million years. Scientists have tried to associate specific geologic features, animals, etc., with each of these divisions. For example,the Alps, Andes, and Himalayas were formed during the Cenozoic Era. During our contemporary Holocene Epoch, which began about 10,000 years ago, the last Ice Age glaciers melted, and the water collected formed the Great Lakes in North America. Streams, glaciers and oceans eroded land to form present day deltas and coastlines. Man developed the early great civilizations in irrigated lands, and ushered in the world in which we live today. The history of the earth fits well its development in four "days" according to Qur'anic verses, esp. 41:9-10, quoted above.

Conclusions

The Qur'anic verses confirm the rationally discovered facts of recent decades, or earlier, concerning the structure of the heavenly bodies. The heavenly bodies were created, and the astronomical and geologic changes occurred, during very long periods of the time called "days" in the Qur'an. There is nothing in common in the ideas and methodology presented in the Qur'an, and those in the mythology, fables and superstitions, and the pseudo-sciences like astrology in the first century A.H./seventh century A.D. The history of the moon and earth known through scientific studies confirm the basic Qur'anic views.

The emphasis in the Qur'an is on observation and rational astronomical studies; this is the Islamic scientific method linked with God and His laws. Later on Europe adopted a reductionist version of it, the secular scientific method.

This chapter has not touched upon the history of Muslim ideas in astronomy, and its place in mankind's history of astronomy. The popular Western writings have been systematic and deliberate denials of medieval Muslim accomplishments, and their borrowing by and continuation in the west. Western writings hold that modern astronomy suddenly began with Copernicus when he went to Italy from his native Poland, and published in 1543 his *Concerning the Revolutions of the Celestial Spheres.* This is wrong on many counts. Copernicus was a student of Muslim astronomy in Italy. Islamic science and learning in all possible disciplines had been diffusing through Spain and Southern Europe, through use of works in arabic and their translations, and by other means of transmission for centuries in the West. The achievements of Copernicus and Tycho Brahe in the tenth century A.H./sixteenth century A.D., and of Kepler and Galileo in the eleventh century A.H./ seventeenth century A.D. were a continuation of the earlier Muslim traditions of scientific studies. The beginnings of "modern" or scientific astronomy must be found in the verses of the Qur'an and its gradual development in the medieval Muslim civilization.

Notes

[1] The concept of "seven heavens" is presented in seven verses: 2:29, Asad n20; 17:44; 23:86; 41:12; 65:12; 67:3; 71:15; and also in reference to "seven paths" in 23:17, and as "the seven firm ones" in 78:12. There are seven verses on the creation of the "heavens and earth" in "six days" by God: 7:54, n43; 10:3; 11:7, n10; 25:59; 32:4; 50:38; and 57:4, nn 1,2.

[2] 'Arsh may mean a house, a throne, and also might, power, sovereignty, dominion, etc.; hence God ascended the 'arsh might mean that He assumed power and government over the universe after creating the heavens and earth. The expression "then God ascended the throne," or "He is established on the throne" occurs in seven verses: 7:54, n43 ; 10:3; 13:2; 20:5; 25:59; 32:54; and 57:4; in all these it is in connection with creation of the universe.

S.v., "Earth", "Solar System", "Space Exploration", "Mythology", "Universe", The World Book Encyclopedia, 1981.

5. Cat's Eye Nebula, a Dying Star

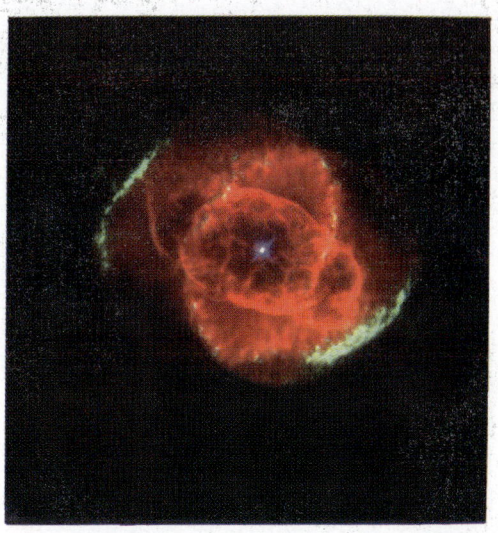

And I call to witness the breaking up of the Stars!

He asks: 'When is that Resurrection Day to be?' But, when the eyesight is by fear confounded, and the moon is darkened, and the sun and the moon are brought together, on that Day will man exclaim, 'Whither to flee?' **(Qur'an 56:75, 75:6-10)**

This colorful image shows the structure of a planetary nebula: expanding clouds of gas thrown off in successive outbursts by a dying star. The elongated shell of glowing gas from a recent outburst is embedded in two gas clouds thrown off in a previous one. The remains of the dying star are its dense helium core. Scientists believe that our sun will die similarly: it will burn up its hydrogen core, swell until it engulfs the Earth, and its cast off shells of gas will continue expanding to turn the sun into a planetary nebula.

6. The Sun - Our Star

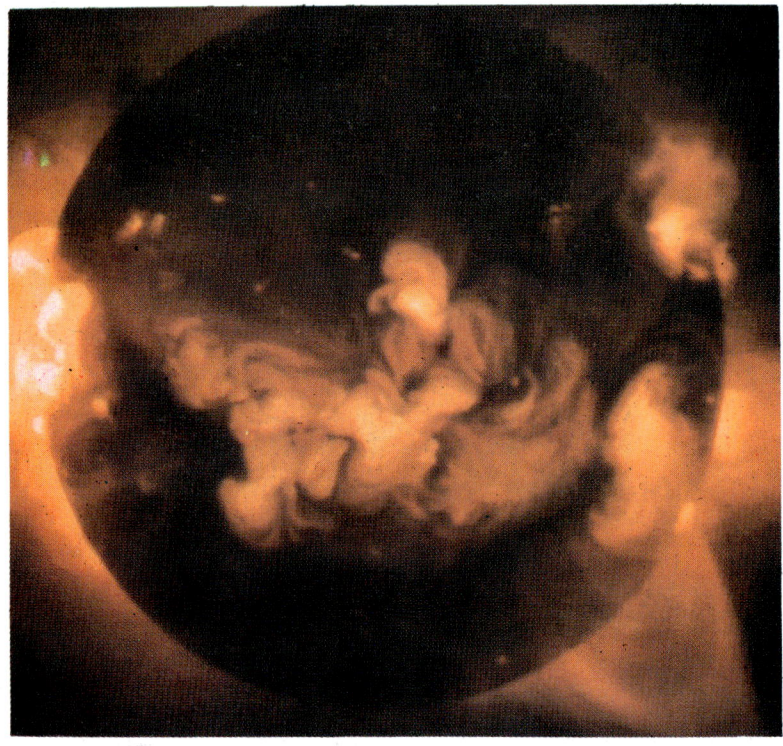

*And He made subservient to you the night and the day and the
sun and the moon; and the planetary bodies are subservient by
His command; herein indeed are signs for sensible people.*
(**Qur'an 16:12**)

This image viewed from space shows the hot, three-dimensional figure
of the corona (Sun's atmosphere) across the full disk of the sun. The
large bright areas are estimated to be regions with over 1 million
degrees C temperature where the sun's magnetic field traps gases. The
dark areas are coronal holes where charged particles (protons and
electrons) called the solar wind originate, and flow past the earth
through the solar system at nearly 700 km/s. The sun's power causes
weather, climate, the seasons, the ocean currents, air's circulation, etc.
God has made it the source of all our food and fossil fuels...*And God
will reward the grateful.* (**Qur'an 3:144**)

7. The Sun - A Nuclear Reactor

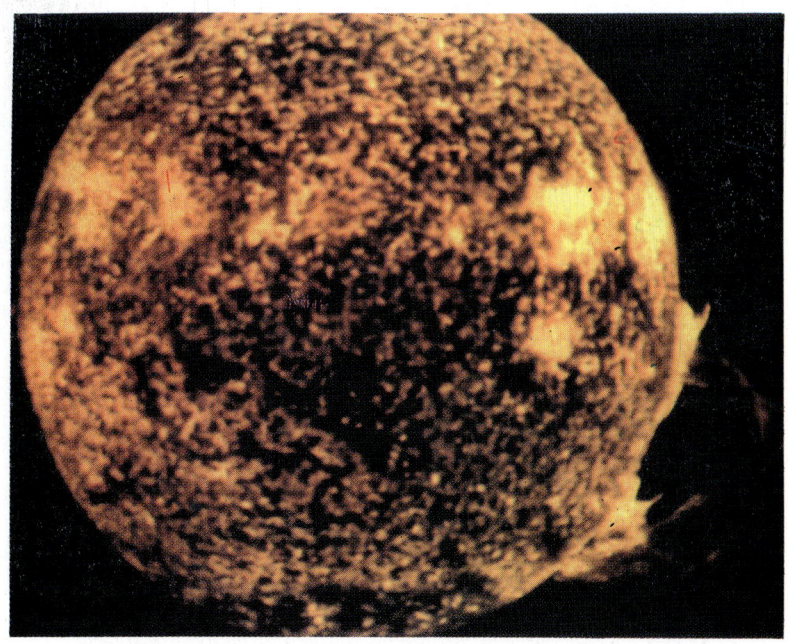

He (God) it is who has made the sun a radiant lamp and the moon a light, and has determined for it phases so that ye might know the number of years and the computations. None of this has God created without the truth. Clearly does He spell the message for people who have knowledge. (**Qur'an 10:5**)

The sun is a nuclear reactor. Fusion of its hydrogen and helium atoms heats its core to an estimated 14 million degrees C, and the corona above sun's surface to 2 million degrees C. Sunspots are the dark, cooler surface regions of 4500 degrees C, whose magnetic fields are thousands of times greater than the rest of the sun's surface. Some charged particles (solar wind) escape the fields, collide with Earth's particles, and produce the aurora.

8. Pluto

*O you who live in communion with invisible beings (jinn) and humans! If you can pass beyond the regions of the heavens and the earth, pass beyond them! You can not pass beyond them save by an authority. (**Qur'an 55:33**)*

This image is an artist's conception of Pluto and its satellite, Charon. Pluto is the smallest, coldest and farthest planet from the Sun at 6 million km. It is the only planet in the solar system not yet visited by a spacecraft. The drawing depicts Pluto's surface as brighter than Charon's. NASA was planning to explore them by launching a spacecraft at high speed in 2000 to reach Pluto by 2010! Space exploration is possible and obligatory in accordance with God's laws of the philosophical and natural sciences.

CHAPTER 6

The Expanding Universe

The Qur'an on the Expanding Universe

And it is We who have built the heaven (as-sama'a)
*with power; and, verily, it is We who are steadily
expanding it* (wa Inna la-musi'un) (51:47, Asad
nn30-31)

*And He applied His design to the skies which were
smoke; and He said to them and the earth, 'Come, both
of you, willingly or unwillingly!' They both responded,
'We do come in obedience.'*
*And He decreed that they become seven heavens in two
days* [eons], *and imparted to each heaven its command.
And He adorned the skies nearest to the earth with
lamps* [stars], *and made them secure. Such is the
determination of the Almighty, the All-knowing.* (41:11-
12, nn11-15)

Do not the Rejecters [disbelievers] *see that the two, the heavens and the earth, were closed up* ["joined, sewed together," as one entity], *then We disjoined the two asunder?...*" (21:30, n38)

Summary and Explanation

The definite noun *as-sama'a* may mean here the sky, the heaven, or the universe. *Musi'un* means one who enlarges or is making of large extent. The prefix *la* provides emphasis and a degree of exaggeration to the noun or adjective that follows it in the sense of "very much" and "very much indeed"; *la-musi'un* may mean in this sentence that God is making the heaven expand very much. The last succinct phrase of the verse may be rendered as: "Indeed, We are very much, or continuously, or steadily expanding" the heaven or universe.

The verses 41:11-12 say that "the heavens" were once a "smoke"; and verse 21:30 states that "the heavens" and "the earth" were once joined together. God disjoined "the heavens" from the earth. In two "days" or eons God created out of that smoke "seven" or several heavens, including the light-giving stars in the heavens nearest to the earth; and He imparted to each heaven its "command" (*amr*) or the laws of their existence.

The subject of this chapter is verse 51:47. After God had created the universe, or the solar system, from the original smoke, when and how did He expand "the heaven" or the universe? Is this process of expansion continuing? Or is it intermittent, occurring at intervals? Is it repetitive, with periods of expansion and contraction? When did the expansion begin, and when will it end? What are the cosmological theories suggested by scientists based on what they have "observed" or come to know in the present state of our knowledge?

Modern Scientific Findings and Theories

Chapter 7 explains "the Big Bang theory," and observation of the phenomenon called the "red shift." The former is supposed to be a massive explosion in the form of a rapidly expanding sphere of radiation called "the primordial fireball" about 13 billion years ago. The fireball changed into radiation and matter. Perhaps a smaller clump of matter formed our solar system about 4.5 billion years ago. The larger clumps of matter formed galaxies which continued to move away from one another. This was suggested by the observation of faint radio waves wherever astronomers pointed radio telescopes. These radio waves are similar to those that would be emitted by an extremely hot object that is moving away from the earth. This reinforced the belief that the universe has been expanding ever since the "Big Bang." It is believed that the galaxies may continue to move apart "for ever." Astronomers also think it is possible that the galaxies may come together again in about 70 billion years. If they do "close up," the material in the universe may explode once again and begin a new universe like the present one!

Scientists do not know if the universe has a size. For example, quasars may be the most distant objects in the universe. These bright objects may be unusual galaxies as much as 10 billion light-years from the earth. This is estimated by the enormous "red shifts" of quasars and other far off galaxies. Red shift is the apparent change in the wave lengths of light as it moves away from the observer. Observation of red shift makes scientists believe that the universe is expanding. Every part of the universe is moving away from every other part. This is the fundamental characteristic of the universe that modern scientists are trying to explain through various cosmological theories.

Most cosmological theories assume that any part of the universe is like any other part that has the same age. The predicted behaviour of the universe is based on two beliefs stemming from Einstein's general theory of relativity: the laws of physics are the same all over the universe; and no signal can travel faster than the speed of light.

Cosmological theories based on these ideas suggest a universe that expands and contracts. Observation of the red shifts of galaxies makes astronomers conclude that the universe is expanding. However, the expansion or contraction of the universe depends on the average density of matter in the universe. This consideration gives rise to three possible models of the universe: an open, a closed or oscillating universe, and a steady state model.

If all the known matter in the universe was spread out evenly, there would be only one atom of hydrogen per 10 cubic yards of space. The universe, then, would be "open": the mutual gravitational attraction among the galaxies would not be strong enough to slow the speed at which they are moving apart much, and the universe would continue to expand indefinitely, approaching zero density in infinite time. All galaxies would recede to an infinite distance.

However, there may be large amounts of matter in the universe that are unknown to scientists. If the density of such matter were just 100 atoms of hydrogen per 10 cubic yards of space, what is believed today to be the critical value, the universe could be said to be "closed": its expansion would slow to a halt due to gravitational force may be after 100 billion years and then actually reverse to contract, ending in a total collapse of the universe into itself. According to some theories, this "closed" universe may then explode again—another "Big Bang"—to produce a new expanding universe. This is the "oscillating" model of the universe.

The "steady state" model is based on the belief that at all times any part of the universe is like all other parts. In this model the decrease of density due to expansion is balanced by creation of new matter condensing into new galaxies that replace those that recede into infinite space. Astronomical findings since 1965 have, however, proved this model to be inadequate.

Some scientists have suggested changes in Einstein's theory of relativity that would predict different things for the expanding universe. To prove their theories, scientists need data like the average density of matter in the universe, its age, the behaviour of red shifts at very large distances, etc. This may be impossible to obtain. Therefore, scientists do not know which of their theories, if any, may be correct.

Notes

S.v., "Milky Way", "Red Shift", "Universe", *The World Book Encyclopedia,* 1981.

CHAPTER 7

The Universe, or the Solar System: Birth and Evolution

The Qur'an on the Birth and Development of the Solar System

Do the Rejecters [disbelievers] not see that the two, heavens and earth were closed up [ritqa, as one entity], then We parted asunder (fa-fataq-na) the two? And We made out of water every living thing. Will they not, then, believe?" (21:30, Asad nn 38, 39)

The above verse 21:30 must be read with the following:

And He applied His design to the skies which were smoke; and He said to them and the earth, 'Come, both of you, willingly or unwillingly!' They both responded, 'We do come in obedience.
And He decreed that they become seven heavens in two

109

days [eons], *and imparted to each heaven its command. And We adorned the skies nearest to the earth with lights, and made them secure; such is the ordination of the Almighty, the All-Knowing.* (41:11-12, nn10-15; cf. 2:29, n20; 15:16-18, nn16f; 37:6-10, n6)

Summary and Explanation

The two key verbs or their derivatives, *ritqa* from *rataqa*, and *fataq* from *fataqa*, each occurs only once in the Qur'an in this verse. *Ritqa* means closed up; sewed up, or together; closed up, without any interstice. *Fataqa* means to slit; rent asunder or open; disjoin, disunite, divide up; unsew, unstitch. "The heavens and the earth" may be understood here to refer to our solar system which is a very tiny part of the "universe."

What are the literal meanings of the key words and the verses above? The answer is: the two separate entities, "the heavens" and "the earth," were once something closed up or joined together; the two were then disjoined. How do we explain these statements through our contemporary knowledge of the astronomical sciences like cosmology and astrophysics? How were the heavens and earth "closed up," "sewed together," or joined "without an interstice"? What were they made up of in that condition? When and how were they disjoined? What were these states of union and separation, and has the universe undergone more than one cycle of being "closed up" and "disjoined"? What changes and processes took place during these states, and how long were they? What is the history of the universe since it was last opened up? How are we supposed to "see" (*tara*, 21: 30), or know, all this? The obvious implication of

110

the latter is that it is possible to observe or know these cosmological phenomena; and it is man's duty to do so. Must the Rejecters of God and Islam, then, become believers based on this cosmological evidence of God's work?

Modern Cosmological Sciences and Theories

Astronomers observed in the early 1900s that the light from stars in distant galaxies was shifted toward the longer, or red wavelengths of the spectrum (color pattern). This is due to the rapid motion of the galaxies away from the earth; they concluded that the universe was expanding. This "red shift" allowed the astronomers to study the speed of the motion of the galaxies at various distances from the earth. They calculated that all galaxies came from one point in the universe about 13 billion years ago; they believed, therefore, that the universe was born 13 billion years ago. They explained these observations through the "Big Bang" theory. The universe was born as a result of an explosion which consisted chiefly of radiation. It formed a rapidly expanding sphere called the "primordial fireball." Later on the fireball changed into matter consisting mostly of hydrogen, and small amounts of helium and other elements. The radiation sphere and matter continued to move away from the point of the Big Bang explosion. In due course the matter broke apart in massive clumps which became galaxies. A part of one such clump became a group of planets, and one star which is the sun; this is our solar system which was formed about 4.5 billion years ago.

Two general theories were proposed until the mid-1900s to explain formation of the solar system. The "monistic theories" suggest that the solar system was formed from one cloud of gas. According to some theories, all parts of the solar system were formed at the same time; other monistic theories suggest that the sun was formed first, and the planets and other objects were formed later from the remaining gas. The "dualistic theories" hold that the solar system was formed when an object passed near the sun; its force of gravity pulled a stream of gas from the sun to form the planets and other objects in the solar system.

Since the 1950s scientists have been learning more and more from space probes and exploration of the moon about meteorites, the moon, the processes of star formation, etc. They have discovered, for example, that the interiors and atmospheres of most of the planets differ greatly from those of the earth.

Conclusion

Modern theories suggest that whatever existed before the "Big Bang" became the "primordial fireball" after the Big Bang; or "the smoke" was perhaps the subsequent cloud of a gas consisting of both radiation and matter; or perhaps it was the clump of gas from which the solar system evolved later on. Whatever the cosmological theories may say in the light of our increasing and changing knowledge, the verses above give the basic idea that "the heavens and the earth" were once "a smoke" (*dukhan*), the two were "closed up" as a single entity, and then they were disjoined to form the sun, the earth, the moon, and other heavenly bodies comprising our solar system and, perhaps, other stars.

Notes

S.v., "Red Shift", "Universe", *The World Book Encyclopedia*, 1981

9. Venus: Topographic Map

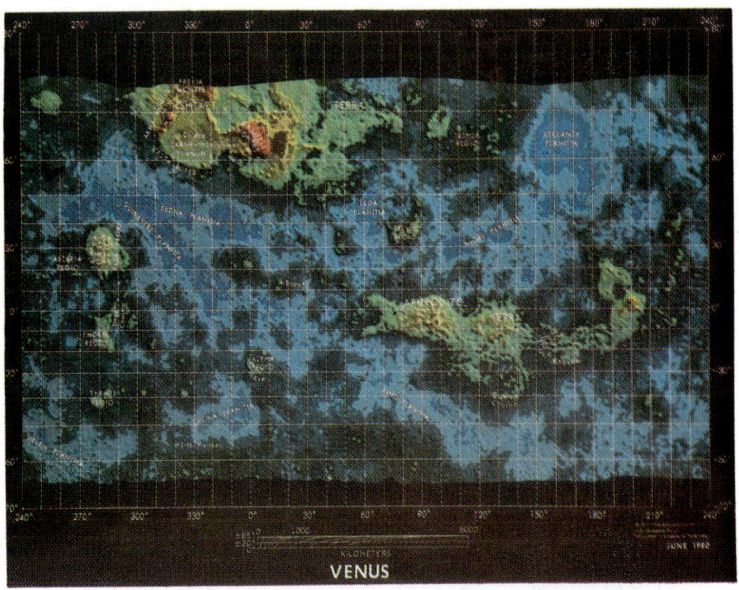

Hallowed is He who has placed in the sky a group of planetary bodies, and has placed among them a lamp and a light-giving moon. **(Qur'an 25:61)**

Scientists have mapped nearly the entire planet based on radar data sent by Pioneer Venus, a NASA spacecraft. Its surface has never been seen because clouds permanently cover Venus. Its topography is shown consisting of highlands (in green, yellow and red), and lowlands (in dark blue). A rolling plain (in light blue and blue-green) covers about 60% of the planet's surface and varies in height by only about 1,000 m.

10. Comet Shoemaker-Levy 9, and Planet Jupiter

Have they not observed how God creates in the first instance, and then brings it forth anew? This, verily, is easy for God! (**Qur'an 29:19**)

This composite photograph was assembled from separate images of Jupiter and the chain of 21 fragments of comet Shoemaker-Levy 9 which stretches across 1.1 million km in space. The comet had orbited Jupiter for dozens of years. Scientists believe that it was broken into pieces, seen in this image, by the gravity of Jupiter when it passed close to it in July 1992. Comets are pieces of dust and ice; they were formed when our solar system was born over 4 billion years ago.

11. Multiple Comet Impact Sites on Jupiter

Do they not, then, see how little of the sky and the earth lies open before them, and how much is hidden from them? If We willed, We could cause the earth to swallow them or fragments from the sky to fall down upon them! In this there is indeed a message for every servant [of God] who turns unto Him. **(Qur'an 34:9)**

Eight impact sites were identified on Jupiter from the collisions of the fragmented comet, Shoemaker-Levy 9. This image was taken on July 22, 1994, before the last fragment entered Jupiter's atmosphere. The impact sites appear as dark smudges which are chemical debris of the fireballs produced by each impact. This comet crash was the first time astronomers predicted that a comet would strike a planet, and then observed it happen. Comets of such size are supposed to strike Jupiter once in a millennium.

12. Asteriods: Ida with its Moon, and Gaspra

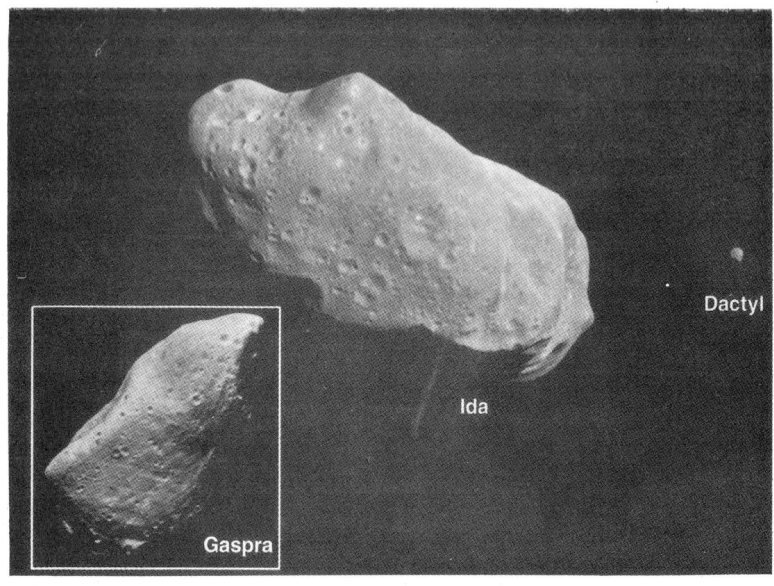

Do you not see that God has made subservient to you what is on earth, and the ship runs upon the sea by His command, and He holds back the sky [celestial bodies] so that it does not fall upon the earth except by His leave? Verily, God is compassionate, merciful, towards men. (**Qur'an 22:65**)

Spacecraft Galileo, launched in October 1989, sent the first ever close-up view of asteroids (minor planets) : Gaspra in October 1991, and Ida and its tiny moon Dactyl in August 1993. They are irregular bodies riddled with craters and fractures. Gaspra was perhaps 97km across during formation of the solar system but now is 19x12x11km after catastrophic collisions with other planetary bodies. Meteoroids, whose sources are mostly asteroids, are called meteorites when they enter earth's atmosphere before burning and can cause disasters if they are large. About 200 million descend daily as meteors which are tiny burnt out particles.

CHAPTER 8

The Sun's Motion

The Qur'an on Sun's Motion

*Alif Lam Mim Ra. These are messages of the Book of
Revelation* [the Qur'an]; *and what has been bestowed
upon you* [O Muhammad] *from on high by your
Sustainer is the truth, yet most people do not believe.
It is God who has raised the heavens without supports
that you could see. And He is established on the throne*
[of His almightiness]; *and He has made the sun and
moon subservient* (saqqara), *each running* (yajri) *its
course for a term set* (li-ajal musamma). *He governs
all that exists. Clearly does He spell out these messages*
(ayat), *so that you might be certain that you are
destined to meet your Sustainer.* (13:1-2; cf. 31:10)

*Do you not observe that it is God who makes the night
grow longer by shortening the day, and He makes the
day longer by shortening the night, and that he has*

made the sun and the moon subservient, each running its course for a set term, and that God is fully aware of all that you do?

Thus it is, because God alone is the Ultimate Truth, so that all that men invoke instead of Him is sheer falsehood; and because God alone is exalted, truly great!" (31:29-30)

And We have set up the sky as a canopy well-secured; and yet they stubbornly turn away from the signs of this.

And it is He who has created the night and the day, and the sun and the moon, all of them floating through space. (21: 32-33)

And they have a sign in the night: We withdraw from it the day, and lo! they are in darkness.

And the sun runs to its point of rest; that is laid down by the will of the Almighty, the All-knowing; and [for] the moon We have determined phases [to traverse] till it becomes like an old date-stalk, dried-up and curved: neither may the sun overtake the moon, nor does the night outrun the day, since all of them float through space. (36: 37-40)

Summary and Explanation

The sun, moon and earth are not stationary. They are "floating" in the "sky" or "the heavens"; they are "running" in subservience to the will or laws of God. They are kept afloat by God by an invisible force. We can ourselves "see" that they are not held up by any visible column or support ('amad). The movements of these planets and stars are for a fixed time (li-ajal musamma); thus their speed, direction, life-span, etc. are pre-determined. The sun and moon are not allowed to overtake or collide with one and another. The sun is moving towards or to (ila) a place or a point of rest (mustaqar); thus its direction, duration, and life are also fixed. All this is the ordination or pre-determination (taqdir) of God. He is the Regulator of these matters. On the basis of these observable facts, or rationally knowable astronomical sciences, it is asserted that these are verses or messages (ayat) of the Book of God, the Qur'an. It was revealed to Muhammad, the Messenger of God; and people must believe in the Day of Judgement when God will put an end to this universe as we know it; and we will be judged for our deeds in life.

What are the "facts" given in these verses that we can know based on our contemporary rational knowledge? What are the conclusions the human mind can deduce from them? And how have they changed from age to age since the Qur'an was revealed?

These verses of the Qur'an were revealed to Muhammad 1400 years ago during the years 13 BH.-10 A.H./A.D. 610-632. What was the state of human knowledge concerning this subject in the Arabian peninsula where Muhammad was born and raised? What were the human ideas then in other nearby and far off societies, and their intellectual legacies? How much agreement and disagreement was there between those human ideas in the first century A.H. / seventh century A.D. and these Qur'anic ideas? And what is the relation between the

Qur'anic astronomical ideas as they are understood today, and modern human knowledge? How can we explain these conflicts and agreements between human knowledge and, on the other hand, the facts and conclusions based on the Qur'an? How did Muhammad know the ideas presented in the Qur'an? Who could have produced the Qur'an, "a transcribed or written book" (*kitab mastur*, 52:2) ? Only in the fourteenth century A.H./twentieth century A.D. do we seem to have "true" knowledge of this subject due to the availability of verifiable data or "scientific evidence."

These and other questions beg for answers from Islamic intellectuals. The following short history of the evolution of rational knowledge on the sun's movements brings out the agreements between modern scientific concepts on the subject and the ideas presented in the Qur'an.

Pre-Qur'anic Views

In the first century A.H./seventh century A.D., the most influential human knowledge in the Near East about the universe was based on Greek astronomy. Ptolemy, who flourished in the second century A.C. in Alexandria, Egypt, presented this in his *Almagest.* He summarized the ideas of earlier Greek astronomers, especially Hipparchus of the second century B.C. The Ptolemaic system was based on a geocentric (earth-centered) theory. Ptolemy had said that the earth is the center of the universe, and it had no motion. The sun, moon, and other bodies were supposed to revolve around the earth along the circumference of a circle called the deferent; their orbits were circles, called epicycles, whose centers would be on the deferent. The Qur'anic verses do not support the Ptolemaic view of the universe.

Modern and Contemporary Sciences and Theories

Copernicus (A.D.1473-1543) published his masterpiece, *Concerning the Revolution of the Celestial Spheres,* in 1543. He presented the view that the earth is a moving planet. People do not feel this motion because they travel with the earth. However, this heliocentric hypothesis made the sun the center of the universe. It proposed that the earth and other planets travel around the sun. This was opposed by Tycho Brahe (d A.D. 1601) because it was not possible then to measure correctly the parallax of stars. Friedrich Bessel (1784-1846) was the first person to publish an authentic measurement of the annual parallax of a star. He proved, thus, the motion of the earth. But this also seemed to support the heliocentric theory.

Only in the middle of thirteenth century A.H./ nineteenth century A.D. did scientists realize that the apparent daily movement of the celestial sphere and its bodies is merely the reflection of the earth's rotation on its own axis. The sun's apparent motion must be attributed to the earth's revolution in its orbit around the sun; the sun appears in different directions due to the earth's position in its orbit.

The discovery of the movement and direction of the sun, our solar system and our galaxy, is a most recent achievement of human thought. It has been built up on a series of discoveries. Galileo saw in A.D.1610 , after the telescope was introduced to astronomy, that the Milky Way Galaxy is a huge gathering of stars; our solar system is a part of this galaxy. In the second decade of the twentieth century, it was estimated that the Milky Way galaxy, which includes about 200 billion stars, has a diameter of about 100,000 light years. A light year is the distance travelled by light in one year when light is travelling at a speed of 300,000 kilometers per second (km/s)! The sun lies nearer to the edge of the Milky Way; it is not the center of this galaxy or the universe as was thought in the heliocentric view.

Other galaxies with spiral arms were discovered in 1925; their stars also seemed to move. An analysis of the motion of stars in our galaxy suggested that the sun revolves in a circular orbit round the galaxy's center at a speed of about 220 km/s to complete a revolution every 200 million years. It was also estimated that the sun moves, in relation to the group of stars near it, at about 19.7 km/s in a direction pointing to the Weger Star in the Lyra Galaxy. This direction is known as the solar apex. Thus the sun too moves in an orbit and a specific direction.

Much progress has been made in astronomical studies during the second half of the fourteenth century A.H./twentieth century A.D. Scientists claimed in 1975 that they had discovered many other galaxies. The speed of our Milky Way galaxy was found to be about 500 km/s. They estimated that the Milky Way Galaxy, including our solar system and billions of other stars, and the Andromeda and other neighboring galaxies, are all running in cosmic space at a speed of 600 km/s approximately. They have a direction which is perpendicular to the line of vision between the solar system and the galaxy's center; it is opposite to the direction of the galaxy's revolution, and above its plane at about 27 degrees. Thus the Milky Way and other galaxies have both a speed and direction.

However, where are our solar system and galaxy, and other galaxies going? What is causing this movement, speed and direction? Scientists have tried to answer these questions by proposing the existence of a secondary movement caused by the "Big Bang." The "Big Bang" is supposed to be a massive release of radiation that caused the beginning of the universe. Another explanation is that there is a "great attracter" constituted by great masses located in some place! A group of researchers announced in 1986 that they had discovered "the great attracter" and its location. They estimated it to be in the direction of the Hydra Centaurus galaxy at a distance which is twice its distance from the earth, i.e., about 200 million light years!

The above summary of recent advances in human knowledge shows that the local system, including our sun, the solar system and our Milky Way galaxy, are in motion. They are speeding in space, perhaps, towards "the great attracter" which is over 200 million light years from the earth. This system is revolving with groups and islands of other galaxies. This motion is supposed to be due to the expansion of the universe and its galactical recession.

The sun's motion towards its solar apex was not known except very recently in this century. The orbital motion of the sun around the galaxy's center, like the moon's movement around the earth, was also discovered recently. These and other recent scientific ideas seem to confirm the basic ideas revealed in the Qur'an.

Conclusions

It is beyond the scope of this book to review the history of Muslim ideas since the Qur'an was revealed. The epicyclic, geocentric, heliocentric and other views had been opposed by Islamic astronomers and other Islamic scholars who were following the guidance of the Qur'an. The non-Muslim scholars of the Middle Ages and later centuries were influenced by this Islamic science. These Islamic scientists did not have the experimental tools and data that became increasingly available later on; they were acting on the basis of their beliefs through a literal reading of the Qur'an as well as their mathematical and experimental studies. The history of the Islamic opposition to Alexandrian, Greek, Hindu and Buddhist Indian, Chinese and other traditions in astronomy and astrology may be studied in the bibliographic references given elsewhere.

Notes

S.v., "Friedrich W. Bessel", "Copernicus", "Galaxy" "Milky Way Galaxy", "Ptolemy", "Solar System", "Sun," "Tycho Brahe", *The World Book Encyclopedia*, 1981.

CHAPTER 9

The Moon:
Its Movement and Light

Introduction

This chapter deals with the Qur'anic verses on movement of the moon and its light. It compares them with man's views when the Qur'an was revealed and according to modern science.

The Qur'an on the Moon as a Moving Satellite of the Sun

And He has made the sun and the moon, both of them constant upon their courses (da'ibin), subservient (saqqara) to you; and He has made the night and the day subservient to you.

And He does give you some thing out of what you may be asking of Him; and should you try to count God's blessings, you could never compute them. [And yet] behold, man is indeed most persistent in wrong doing, stubbornly ingrate! (14:33-34, Asad n 46)

It is God who has raised the heavens without any supports that you could see, and He is firmly established on the throne [of His almightiness]; *and He has made the sun and moon subservient, each running for a term set. He plans the commands* (or, "He manages, *yudabbir,* the affair, *amr"*). *Clearly does He spell out these messages so that you might be certain that you are destined to meet your Sustainer.* (13:2, nn 4-6)

He makes the night grow longer by shortening the day, and He makes the day longer by shortening the night; and He has made the sun and moon subservient, each running (yajri) for a term set. Thus is God, your Sustainer; unto Him belongs all dominion whereas those whom you invoke instead of Him do not own so much as the husk of a date-stone! (35:13; also 31:29 and 39:5 for repetition of the phrase, *"and He has made the sun and the moon subservient ... for a term set."*)

The Qur'an on the Moon as a Light *(Nur)* and Light-giving *(Munir)* Planet

He it is who has made the sun [the source of] *a radiant light* (diya') *and the moon a* [reflected] *light* (nur), *and He has determined for it phases so that you might know how to compute the years and to measure* (hisab). *None of this has God created without truth. Certainly does He spell out these messages unto people of knowledge."* (10:5, Asad nn 10 & 11)

Do you not see how God has created seven heavens in full harmony with one another, and has set up within

126

them the moon as a light [reflected, *nur*], *and set up the sun as a lamp (siraj). (71:16)*
Hallowed is He who has set up in the skies great constellations (buruj), and has placed among them a lamp (siraj) and a light-giving (munir) moon. (25:61, Asad n48)

Consider the sun and its radiant brightness (duha-ha), and the moon as it follows it (tala-ha)!
Consider the day as it reveals it [the world], *and the night as it veils it* [in darkness]*!. (91: 1-4, nn1-3)*

Summary and Explanation

The above verses are cited to focus on only two topics. Is the moon stationary or in motion? What is its relation to the other heavenly bodies like the sun and the stars? Is there a difference between the lights of the moon and the sun? What is the significance of the different descriptions of their light used in the Qur'an? What were the views of man in Near Eastern thought and other traditions before and during the times when the Qur'an was revealed about 1400 years ago? What are the modern scientific views on these topics?

The moon is a part of our Milky Way galaxy and its solar system; these modern terms are subsumed in Qur'anic generalizations like the "skies" and *buruj* (groups of stars and planets). They were all created by God, and are subservient (*saqqara, musaqqarat*) to God's laws of astronomy and moral will (*amr*); the moon has been made subservient to man too (7:54; 13:2; 14:33; 16:12; 29:61; etc.). The functions and uses of the moon include providing light, and direction for travelers; reckoning (*hisab*) time and seasons; and providing the "signs or messages" (*ayat*) of God's existence and His laws of nature (6:96; 55:5; etc.).

The sun and the moon are often linked together in the Qur'an, sometimes with other stars, in reference to their movements in the heavens. The moon, sun, and other heavenly bodies are "floating" (*yasbahun*) in the sky (36:40); they are constantly moving fast, or "running" (*yajri*). The motion of the moon and sun is described also as *da'ibin;* the term literally means that they are both "laboring or toiling, hard and continuously, subject to weariness and fatigue." These terms must be understood also as their creation, movement in space, beginning, and eventual end without deviation from God's prescribed laws and His purposeful will. All this is God's pre-determination *(taqdir) "... and the sun and the moon are* [according to] *a reckoning. This is the taqdir of the Almighty, the All-knowing"* (6:96).

This ordering (*amr*) and governance (*musaqqarat*) of the planetary system is known to men of reason and knowledge; if they are sincere in their professional knowledge, they will admit that God is the Nourisher, Manager, etc. (*rab*) of the universe.

Modern Scientific Knowledge and Theories

Contemporary human knowledge tells us that the moon revolves around the earth in its own orbit once every 27.3 days. It deflects by 13 degrees every day; this delays its appearance on the horizon by about 51 minutes per day. The moon also revolves on its axis once every 27.3 days; this is the period of its revolution round the earth too. Thus the moon has a compound motion; one movement is transferential, and the other is a spindle-like movement around its axis.

Modern scientific knowledge, thus, confirms the basic facts of astronomy revealed in the Qur'an; these ideas were not known to mankind through rational knowledge. The Muslims of earlier centuries also could not explain that the "floating" or "swimming" (*yasbahun*) of the sun and the moon in the sky referred to their revolution and orbiting in space according to certain exact, fixed, and pre-determined numbers (*bi-husban*). A very minute change in the speed or orbit of the moon, or any planet, could cause massive changes, disasters, and the destruction of the universe as we know it. God will one day cause the moon to be cleft asunder (54:1), the moon will cease to shine, and the sun and the moon will be joined together (75:8-9). Thus the appointed life-time (*ajal musammah*) of the solar system will come to its end. Modern science also claims that there was a beginning for our solar system, and there will be an end to it. It was neither timeless nor will it be eternal.

A distinction is made according to Arabic philology between the lights produced by the sun and the moon. The sun is a "lamp," *siraj*, which consumes a fuel to produce heat and light; it produces *diya'*, "a light which subsists by itself, as that of the sun and fire." The sun glows by "its own light," (*diya-ha*). The moon is a *munir*, "one that emanates *nur*"; the latter is a" light that subsists by some other thing."

The moon "follows it," (*tala-ha*), that is, the sun. This may be explained in terms of our knowledge of the solar system. The sun is the center of our solar system. Its mass is more than 750 times that of all the nine planets of the solar system. This huge mass creates the gravitation that makes the heavenly bodies in the solar system, including the moon and the earth, travel around the sun. Thus the moon and the earth are "subservient," *(saqqara)*, and toiling obediently *(dayibin)* around the sun. The moon merely reflects the sun's light; it moves in an orbit determined largely by the sun's gravity.

Modern science tells us that moons, unlike the sun and other stars, do not produce light; the moons reflect the rays of their suns. Our sun is a fireball that glows with "its own light," *(diya-ha)*; the sun produces energy from thermonuclear reactions near its center that change hydrogen into helium.

The moons are solid bodies that differ in composition from one planet to another, or from one moon to another. Modern astronomers, and those who landed on the moon, have discovered that our moon is a rocky body. It has a low hardness to a depth of 20 centimeters. The deeper we go, the harder it becomes. The rocks of the moon are remarkable for their gray color; they are similar to earth's basalt and granite. The moon's soil that reflects the sunlight varies in color from dark to pitch dark. Moon rocks contain transparent crystals which reflect like quartz, or groups of fine and intermediate particles like crushed rocks of various kinds, different metals, and glassy rocks. Moon rocks and moon dust have metals like monazite, organic iron, clino-pyroxene, etc. Thus man's landing on the moon, the exploration of its surface, and analysis of the composition of moon's rocks have provided proof of how and why the moon is a *munir* that gives light through reflection of the sun's rays.

Notes

S.v., "Moon", "Space Travel", *The World Book Encyclopedia*, 1981.

13. Moon Landings

Do you not see that before God prostrate themselves all that are in the heavens and all that are on earth, and the sun, and the moon, and the heavenly bodies, and the mountains, and the trees, and the beasts, and many among human beings, and for many the punishment is incumbent. And he whom God scorns has none to bestow honor on him. Verily, God does what He wills. **(Qur'an 22:18)**

God Almighty has made it a duty for man to "see", "observe", "travel", etc. to gain knowledge of how God created the universe and made its functioning and use subservient to His moral and physical laws. In July 1969 the moon became the first object in space to be visited thus by men. However, this task was performed within a secular rather than an Islamic worldview through the science and technology developed by a non-Islamic country, the U.S.A., by secularized and non-Muslim U.S. astronauts. A lunar rover was first used by U.S. Apollo 15 astronauts in July 1971.

14. First Lunar Expeditions

And thus if you ask them, 'Who created the heavens and the earth, and made the sun and the moon subservient?,' they will answer, 'God.' How perverted, then, are they? (**Qur'an 29:61**)

The moon shows the same face as it orbits Earth. The 2/3 region at the right is part of the side never seen from Earth. The dark regions are the maria covered with basalt lava flows; the light ones are lunar highlands made of older rocks containing large craters. U.S.S.R. spaceships first hit the moon in 1959 and sent pictures of its far side. U.S. Apollo 11 and 12 astronauts landed on the moon in 1969, explored it, collected samples, took photographs and set up scientific experiments. Since then much has been learnt about its geophysics and other characteristics.

15. Lunar Surface

I swear by the sunset's afterglow, and the night and what it unfolds, and the moon as it grows to fullness, that ye are bound to move onward from stage to stage. What, then, is amiss with them that they will not believe, and when the Qur'an is read unto them, they do not fall down in prostration? (**Qur'an 84:16-20**)

Scientists surmise that the moon's exterior was molten rock early in its life, about 4.4 billion years ago. As it cooled and solidified it was bombarded by asteroids until 4 billion years ago; this created its rugged highlands. Extensive volcanism then filled many giant craters and produced the maria until three billion years ago. Since then occasional meteorites have changed the surface, and solar wind slowly turns over the lunar soil.

16. The Earth

And Thy Sustainer said unto the angels; 'Behold, I am about to establish upon the earth vicegerent.' They said: 'Will Thou place on it such as will spread corruption thereon and shed blood, whereas it is we who extol Thy limitless glory, and praise Thee, and hallow Thy name?' [God] said: 'Verily, I know that which you do not know.' (**Qur'an 2:30**)

Our planet is easily identified from space by its blue waters and white clouds. Surrounded by an atmosphere of 78% nitrogen and 21% oxygen, and a temperature range of + 140 to -130 degrees F, it is the only planet with life as we know it. Its molten iron-nickel core and fast spin create a magnetic field which shields it from solar radiation and meteors.

CHAPTER 10

Evolution of the Stars, the Sun, and the End of the Earth

The Qur'an on the Birth and End of Stars, and End of the Earth

Nay! I call to witness the Day of Resurrection! ... But [on that Day,] when the eyesight is confounded, and the moon is darkened, and the sun and the moon are brought together (jumi'a) — on that Day will man exclaim, 'Whither to flee?' But nay: no refuge! With thy Sustainer, on that Day, the journey's end will be. (75:1, 7-12, Asad n3; see also 20:105-107, n90)

And they estimate not God with an estimation due to Him. The whole earth will be as a [mere] handful to Him on Resurrection Day, and the heavens will be rolled up in His right hand: limitless is He in His glory and

135

sublimely exalted above anything to which they may ascribe a share in His divinity! (39:67, n66)

On that Day [of Resurrection] *We shall roll up the skies as written scrolls are rolled up; [and] as We brought into being the first creation, so We shall return it* (nu'iduhu) — *a promise which We have willed upon Ourselves: for, behold, We are able to do* [all things]. (21:104)

[God's promise will be fulfilled] *on the Day when the earth shall be changed into another earth, as shall be the heavens, and when* [all mankind] *shall appear before God, the One who holds absolute sway over all that exists.* (14:48, Asad n63)

When the sun is shrouded in darkness, and when the stars lose their light, and when the mountains are made to vanish, ... and when the seas boil over, ... and when the heaven is laid bare, and when the blazing fire is kindled bright, and when paradise is brought into view, [on that Day] *every human being will come to know what he has prepared* [for himself]. (81:1-3, 6, 11-14)

When the sky is cleft asunder (anfatarat), *and when the stars are scattered, and when the seas burst beyond their bounds, and when the graves are overturned, every human being will comprehend what he has sent ahead and what he has held back* [in this world]. (82:1-5, nn1,2)

When the sky is split asunder (anshaqqat), *obeying its*

Sustainer, as in truth it must; and when the earth is extended (maddat), *and casts forth whatever is in it, and becomes utterly void, obeying its Sustainer, as in truth it must,* [then] *O man, you that has, verily, been toiling towards your Sustainer in painful toil, then shall you meet Him!* (84:1-6)

Consider the star when it is destroyed (hawa, destroyed, blown off, falls, disappears, etc.) (53:1,n1)

Summary and Explanation

There are many verses on the transformations that the "heavens" will go through before the ultimate "ending" that God has determined for them. Only a few verses are quoted above. These refer to the "heavens" and stars in general, but the sun, the moon, and the earth in particular. The "day" refers also in Arabic idiom to very short as well as extremely long periods of time; it also means the Day of Resurrection.

The references to astronomical and geophysical phenomena above may be understood by raising questions, and then seeking answers from our contemporary scientific knowledge. When and how will the sun and the moon be joined together (jumi'a)? What is meant by the earth becoming a "handful" to God, and He will fold or roll up "the heavens"? When and how will the sun lose its light to be engulfed in darkness, and why should, then, the stars lose their light? The derivatives, anshaqqah, etc., are used in several verses. God will split, cleave, or rent asunder the skies together with the clouds (25:25), the sky or heaven (69:16; 84:1), the earth (50:44; 19:90), and the moon (54:1).

There will come a "day" on which "the earth is crushed with crushing upon crushing" (89:21): "the earth and the mountains will be crushed with a single crash" (into dust, powder, crumble, *dakka*, 69:16). Some day "the star" will be destroyed (53:1) and other stars will be "scattered"; the oceans will heat up, boil, burn, and overflow (52:6; 81:6); the earth will quake (22:1; 99:1), perhaps due to volcanic eruptions and earthquakes, and it will be "extended or stretched out" (84:3).

Dihan (55:37) literally means freshly tanned leather, sediment of olive oil, etc. This verse perhaps refers to the changing colors of "the sky," or the whole solar system, when it is "split asunder." It will "become like" *dihan*, reddish, when it is engulfed in the "fire" to become, once again, a cosmic cloud and gases, "smoke" (*dukhan*, 44:10). This is the way it was when God began the birth of the "universe" at the first instance; it was "smoke" (41:11). "Then," once again, He shall "repeat it," "return it," or "restore it" (*yu'iduhu*, 10:4; *nu'iduhu*, 34:39). Thus "the earth will be changed into another earth as shall be the heavens"; the universe, and the solar system, will not be as we know them now. Briefly, then, how does God make the stars including the sun, and the whole solar system, be born, change, die, and be reborn? What is our contemporary human understanding of these phenomena?

Contemporary Theories: Star-Formation and Eschatology (End of the World)

Astronomers believe that a star is initially an interstellar cloud of gas and dust. This may be the remnants of a former star or a cloud thrown out of the surface of rotating stars.

The cloud may contract to form a ball during millions of years as gravity pulls it together. The gas pressure at the center of the ball and its temperature too increase. Nuclear fusion begins at about 2 million °F. The hydrogen begins to change into helium and produces nuclear energy. The energy heats the gas surrounding the center. The gas shines; and a star has been born. Stars are divided by size into five groups: supergiants, giants, medium sized stars (like the sun), dwarfs, and neutron stars.

Scientists believe that the sun was born from a similar rotating cloud in the Milky Way galaxy. The sun is a medium-sized star about 4.5 billion years old. It has enough hydrogen to produce energy to probably shine another 5 billion years. Thereafter the sun will begin to shrink, become hotter at the center and expand; this will increase its surface area, release more energy and thus make it slightly cooler at the surface. The sun might expand 30-40 million miles to approach Mercury which is its nearest planet; it would be a "red giant star." Astronomers believe that the sun will shrink, while using up its energy, till it has reached the size of a "white dwarf." It will give off huge amounts of gases in violent explosions as it changes from a red giant to a white dwarf. The latter is a star's final stage of life. During billions of years as a white dwarf, the sun would use up all its energy, lose all its heat, and become a "black dwarf."

What are the consequences for the earth of the changes in the life cycle of the sun? When the sun expands to become a red giant, and approaches the earth, the earth's temperature will be too high to sustain life. For this or any other reason, as the sun comes closer to the earth, one can visualize the rising temperatures causing the oceans to boil and burst beyond their boundaries, as predicted in the Qur'an. If the sun grew to be the size of the "supergiant star," Betelgeuse, it would engulf the planets Mercury, Venus, Earth and Mars. When this occurs some "day," the sun would be joined with the moon too. If the sun expands and comes near the orbit of Mars, its flames would have engulfed the earth and the moon. As a white dwarf, the sun would be the size of the earth. When the sun becomes a black dwarf, the planets in the solar system would be cold and dark. The gases in the earth's atmosphere, if there are any, would have frozen onto the earth's surface. Scientists can not predict what sequences, and what scenario, the end of the solar system would take. However, the Qur'anic eschatology does encompass the modern scientific explanations todate.

Notes

S.v., "Earth", "Solar System", "Sun", Stars", *The World Book Encyclopedia,* 1981.

CHAPTER 11

Atmosphere and Space: Heavens One Above the Other

Introduction

There are some plausible explanations from contemporary science for the only two verses on God creating "seven heavens one above the other," and the other related verses. "Heavens" might mean any regions in the universe, from above the earth to the farthest imaginable areas away from the earth; however, much of our discussion is applied to the earth's atmosphere. "Seven" here means many, several, or any plurality. The Arabic word for "one above the other" also means storeys, as well as harmony, likeness, etc. In 23:17 "tracts" could be replaced by roads, orbits, or paths.

The Quran on "Seven Heavens One Above the Other"

Do you not see how God has created the seven heavens one above the other?
And He made the moon therein a light, and made the sun a lamp? (71:15-16)

Blessed is He in Whose hand is the Kingdom... Who created the seven heavens one above the other. You can see no incongruity in the creation of the Beneficent. Then look again: Can you see any disorder? Then turn the eye again and again— your look will return to you confused while it is fatigued. (67:1, 3-4)

And indeed We have made above you seven tracts — and never are We heedless of creation (23: 17)

Summary and Explanation

The above verses assert that God is the creator of many heavens one above the other. The emphasis is on the characteristics of these heavenly regions as we go above the earth. There is order and harmony among these vast expanses of space reflecting the great intelligence of God, who is always in full control over their purposeful functioning. Human reason is capable and required to "observe" and gain knowledge of "how" God has created these many heavens one above the other; we will never discover any defect in their creation and function. We will soon realize the limits and inadequacy of our faculties.

Modern Scientific Knowledge and Theories

The above verses prompt us to raise some questions. Does our contemporary science confirm or deny the existence of various distinct regions in the universe, space, the earth's atmosphere, etc.? Are these really one above the other over the earth? Are there limitations on man's knowability of these heavens? What are the criteria for their classification? How are these different from each other? In what ways are they alike, and in harmony with each other?

1. Space as "Seven Heavens one Above the Other"

The "seven heavens created one above the other" may be expl ined through our contemporary knowledge of space science. The earth's atmosphere, or air, extends to about 100 miles above the earth. The plentiful air near the earth's surface becomes thinner and thinner higher above its surface. "Space" is said to begin thereafter, where the atmosphere is too thin to influence objects moving through it.

The atmosphere beyond 100 miles above the earth comprises widely scattered atoms, molecules of gases, and radiation. The radiation mostly consists of electrons, protons, and subatomic particles carrying electric charges. These particles are trapped by the earth's magnetic field in a part of the atmosphere called the magnetosphere.

The space between the moon and earth is termed cislunar space. The region in which their gravities are effective, about a million miles from the earth, is called translunar space.

Interplanetary space, the space between planets, is controlled by the sun's gravity. It ends about 50 billion miles from the earth where the sun's gravity is not effective. Vast distances separate the planets. Venus, the closest planet, is about 25 million miles from the earth; the sun is 93 million miles away.

Interstellar space is the distance between stars. The nearest star to Earth, Proxima Centauri, is over 25 trillion miles away. To cover such a distance, man would have to travel a lifetime at about the speed of light. The space between galaxies, intergalactic space, is too great a distance to imagine; it seems never to end. The sun and billions of stars make up one giant galaxy. As far as man has been able to see with the largest telescopes, countless other galaxies appear scattered throughout space.

2. Earth's Atmospheric Regions as "Heavens One Above Another"

Modern astronomy has divided the atmosphere of the earth and the space beyond it into four layers. This is based on the changes in temperature and other parameters as we move up over the earth.

The *troposphere* is the region next to the earth's surface where the temperature ceases to decrease; this is 3-4 degrees F per 1000 feet increase in altitude. It extends about 6 miles over the North and South poles, and about 10 miles over the equator. It contains most of the air, dust and moisture of the atmosphere. Clouds, weather, and the most rapid temperature changes are confined to the troposphere; its upper level is the tropopause.

The *stratosphere* is the region whose lower layer has a nearly constant temperature, but in its upper layer the temperature increases with altitude. It extends from the troposphere to about 30 miles above the earth. At its top, which is the stratopause, it is about 28 degrees F; its lower 15 miles is about -67 degrees F over the United States. The upper layer is warmed up as the sun's rays strike the ozone in this layer.

The *mesosphere,* extending from about 30 to 50 miles above the earth, is the region in which the air temperature decreases from about 28 degrees F to about -135 degrees F near its top, the mesopause. The lowest temperatures in the atmosphere occur in it.

The *thermosphere* continues far into space from about 50 miles to 400 miles above the earth. With very thin air the thermosphere is fully exposed to the sun's radiation; hence the temperature rises rapidly, reaching to over 2700 degrees F in the thermopause which is a layer of uniform temperature. In this layer ultraviolet radiation, x-rays and showers of electrons from the sun ionize the atmosphere. These ionized layers can then conduct electricity and reflect radio waves. These layers within the thermosphere are also called the *ionosphere.* The *ionosphere* enables long-range radio communication without satellites because radio waves can be reflected back to earth thousands of miles away from their source. The *exosphere* is the outermost region of the earth's atmosphere (400-6000 miles) from where molecules escape to outerspace; it has so little air that almost no resistance is offered there to satellites or spacecraft orbiting the earth.

Conclusions

The many heavens one above the other could be described as the earth's atmosphere, and the cislunar to intergalactic spaces. This classification is based on the gravity and other characteristics of the heavenly bodies in the universe as we go towards the farthest outer space. These heavens could also be the earth's atmospheric regions and sub-regions characterized by plentiful to rare air. These are the troposphere and tropopause to thermosphere, thermopause, ionosphere, and exosphere.

These heavens have, at varying distances above the earth, distinct properties of astrophysics, meteorology, hydrology, etc. Man is required to gain knowledge of them through the characteristic Qur'anic style. We are asked: "Have you not seen how God created the seven heavens one above the other ...?" It is only with "authority," perhaps through knowledge and application of the scientific-technological and the socio-humanistic sciences, that man can and should travel in the atmospheric and space regions, avoid the "flames and sparks," understand the limits and possibilities, and recognize God's physical and moral laws.

Modern science recognizes, as stated in 67:3f above and 55:33ff below, man's abilities, limitations, and impossibilities in travelling to the different spaces, comprehending what might be in those heavens, impacting upon them, and receiving benefits and harm through these regions.

O assembly of jinn and men! If you are able to pass through the regions of the heavens and the earth, then pass through. You cannot pass through but with authority ... The flames of fire and sparks of brass will be sent upon you then you will not be able to defend yourselves. Which, then, of the bounties of your Nourisher will you deny? **(5:33, 35f)**

Notes

S.v., "Air", "Atmosphere", and "Space Travel: What is Space", *The World Book Encyclopedia*, 1981.

17. Earth's Biosphere: The First Image

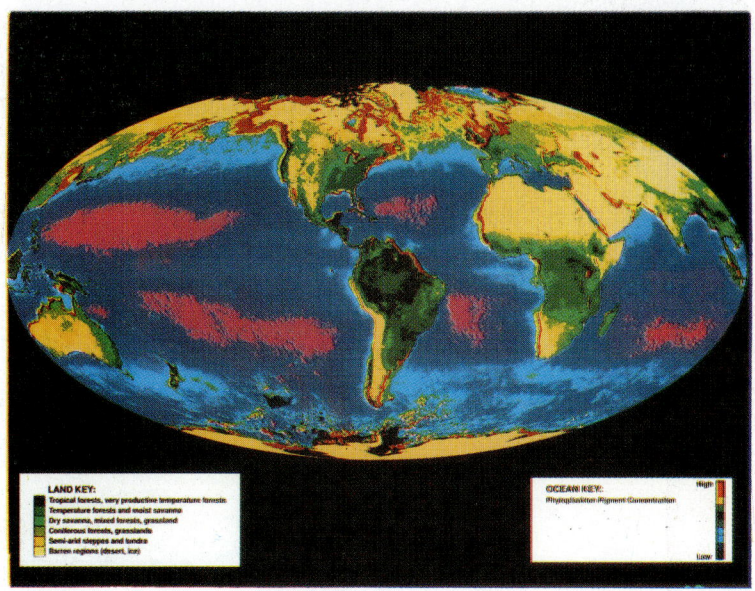

And do not spread corruption on Earth after it has been so well ordered, and call unto Him with fear and longing. Verily, God's grace is near unto the doers of good. **(Qur'an 7:56)**

This illustration, produced by NASA's Mission to Planet Earth program, combined data from two satellites to study Earth as a complete environmental system. The ocean portion, a composite of over 66,000 images collected during 1978-86, indicates the distribution and abundance of phytoplankton. The land vegetation image is a composite of three years' data, 1981-84, collected during 15,000 orbits of a satellite.

18. Earth's Atmospheric Layers, and Space

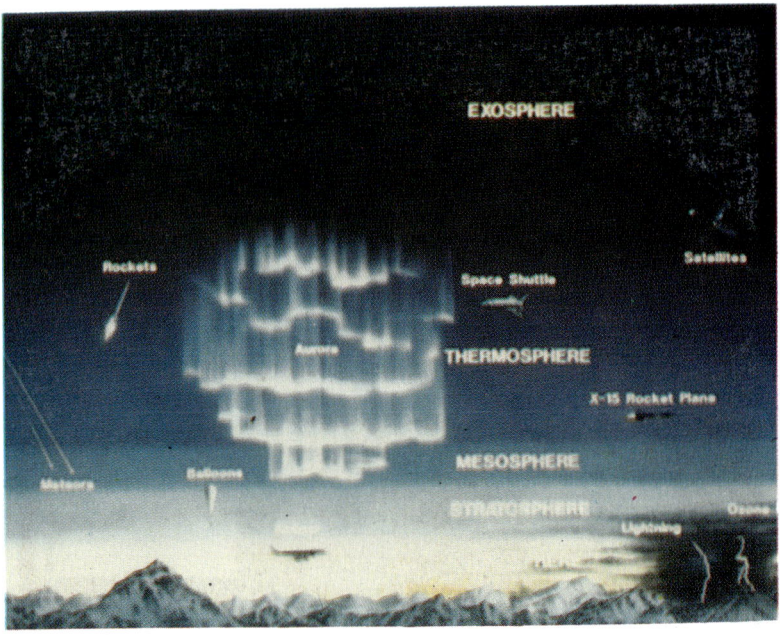

Do you not see how God has created seven (many) heavens one above the other? And He set up within them the moon as a light, and He set up the sun as a lamp? **(Qur'an 71: 15-16)**

Earth's atmosphere is divided into several layers. Troposphere: from surface to 6-10 miles above the Earth. Stratosphere: from 6-10 to about 30 miles. Mesosphere; from 30-50 miles. Mesosphere; from 30-50 miles to region with the lowest temperature of about -135 degree F. Thermosphere: from 50 miles to a region with temperature rising rapidly to over 2700 degrees F. Exosphere: outermost region of Earth's atmosphere with little air. "Space" is defined to begin about 100 miles above the Earth where the air is too thin to offer resistance. Other layers include: thermopause (layer of about 2700 degrees F uniform temperature); and biosphere near the earth's surface.

19. Jet Stream Cirrus, Saudi Arabia

Verily, in the creation of the heavens and the earth, and the difference of night and day, and the ships that run upon the sea with what is useful for mankind, and the water which God sends down from the sky, giving life thereby to the earth after its death, and dispersing all kinds of creatures therein, and in the change of winds, and the clouds obedient between the sky and the earth: are signs for people who have sense. **(Qur'an 2:164)**

A westerly jet stream produces the "roll clouds" stretching from Sudan to Saudi Arabia across the Red Sea. They are a narrow, contained band of cirrus clouds sculpted into tight rolls by air currents from the jet stream. The crest to crest spacing of the cloud bands is used to calculate the velocity of the jet stream.

20. Unique Cloud Lanes, Oman

It is God who sends forth the winds so that they raise a cloud, whereupon He spreads it over the sky as He wills, and causes it to break up so that you see rain issue from within it. And when He causes it to fall upon whomever He wills of His servants, lo! they rejoice; though before that, even before it was sent down upon them, they were in despair! **(Qur'an 30: 48-49)**

These wispy rows of cloud, "cloud lanes," have been recognized as a landmark by successive crews in space shuttle spacecrafts. The clouds are created by a small vortex in the low-level wind current. The air current may have been subjected to heating from the Somali current, but there is little difference between the ocean and atmosphere temperatures. This unique cloud formation is virtually constant at certain times of the year off Oman.

21. Hurricane Bonnie, Atlantic Ocean

Or can you feel secure that He who is in heaven will not let loose against you a stormwind, whereupon you would come to know how My warning was? **(Qur'an 67:17)**

A hurricane, several hundred miles in diameter, is an area of low air pressure that God forms over oceans in tropical regions. Driven by the sun's heat, it produces winds upto 150 mph, heavy rain, huge waves, and can cause death and destruction. Called a typhoon in the North Pacific Ocean, and a cyclone in the South Pacific and Indian Oceans, they occur more than five times annually in certain regions. This hurricane, about 800 km from Bermuda, has a well developed eye. The eye, about 20 miles in diameter, is a calm area in the centre around which storm-clouds swirl carrying the strongest winds and heaviest rain.

22. Dendritic Drainage Pattern, Arabian Peninsula

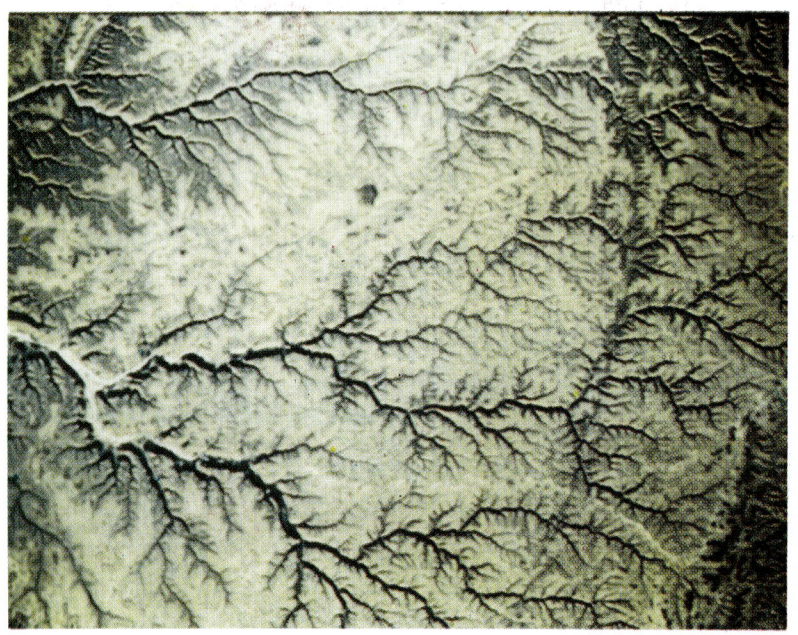

And We send water from the sky in accordance with a measure, and then We cause it to settle in the earth and, verily, We are able to make it withdraw into it. **(Qur'an 23:18)**

This dendritic (tree-like) drainage pattern is from al-Rub'a al-Khali (lit. the Empty Quarter), one of the world's great sand seas in Saudi Arabia. Geologists think that when the earth emerged from the last Ice Age, al-Rub'a al-Khali, like the Sahara, was a savannah grassland with a temperate climate and higher rainfall than now. This pattern was carved by the run-off from the coastal mountains of Yemen. When God changed the climate, this area became an exceptionally arid desert, and the pattern became fossilized.

CHAPTER 12

The Atmosphere: Earth's Protective Roof

Introduction

The focus of this chapter is the assertion in the Qur'anic verses that God created for the earth a protective or guarded roof. This roof or canopy is raised high (52:5). The earth's atmosphere and nearer space, "the lower heaver", may be understood to be that protective roof, guard, or shield over the earth. What forces and phenomena are providing this protection, for whom, and against what? Such questions are raised and their modern scientific explanations provided below.

The Qur'an on Earth's Protective Roof

And We have made the sky a guarded canopy (a roof protected); *yet they turn away from its Signs...*(21:32)

Then He directed Himself to the heaven and it was a smoke, so He said to it and to the earth: 'Come both,

willingly or unwillingly'. They both said: 'We do come in willing obedience.'
So He completed them as seven heavens in two days, and revealed in every heaven its affair. And We adorned the lower heaven with lights, and [provided it] with guard (protection). Such is the determination of the Mighty, the Knowing. (41:11-12)

Surely We have adorned the lower heaven with an adornment, the stars,
And [there is] a guard against every rebellious satan. (37:6-7; cf. 15:16f, and 67:5)

By the mountain; By a Book Inscribed, In a parchment unfolded; By the much-frequented House; By the canopy raised high; And the ocean filled with swell. Verily, the chastisement of your Nourisher will come to pass; There is none [who] can avert it. (52: 1-8)

Summary and Explanation

The basic ideas in the verses are that God has made the sky a guarded and protected roof for the earth. The "lower heaven" might mean the regions of space nearer to the earth where there are easily visible stars. We might interpret the references to guard or protection in two ways. The earth itself is protected by its "roof." The earth's atmosphere and regions of space nearer to the earth are also protected. The "rebellious satan" may mean objects and forces in space, and humans like astrologers, who would go against the natural laws or moral purposes prescribed by God.

Some questions we might ask are: Does our contemporary scientific knowledge provide evidence that the earth, its atmosphere, and space beyond the atmospheric regions are well-protected? What are the hazards to them, and to life on Earth? How do we explain the "roof" for the earth? Another chapter discussed the "seven" or many heavens one above the other covering the earth. What is the function of these heavens, as layers of air and nearer regions of space, in providing protection for the earth and its creatures?

Modern Scientific Explanations and Theories

Chapter 11 mentioned the regions and sub-regions of the earth's atmosphere, and space beyond it which has no air. The four layers and sub-regions of the atmosphere, with their characteristics, are:

Troposphere: 6-10 miles over the earth; contains most of the atmospheric air offering the highest air resistance; temperature changes rapidly, decreasing 3-4 °F per 1000 feet elevation.

Stratosphere: from 6-10 miles to about 30 miles above the earth; in its upper 15 mile layer temperature increases with altitude, it is about 28 °F at its top; there is ozone in this layer.

Mesosphere: from 30-50 miles above the earth; region of lowest temperature which decreases from 28 °F to -135 °F near its top.

Thermosphere: from 50 miles to far into space; region of thinner and thinner air; temperature rises rapidly to over 2700 °F in thermopause which is its upper region; exosphere, its outermost region of very little air, offers almost no air resistance.

"Space" begins about 100 miles above the earth where the air is too thin to offer any resistance. The space divisions are:

Cislunar space: space between the earth and moon.

Translunar space: Upto a million miles from the earth, region in which gravities of earth and moon are effective.

Interplanetary (between planets) *space*: ends about 50 billion miles from earth where sun's gravity ends.

Interstellar (between stars) *space:* star nearest to earth is about 25 trillion miles away.

Intergalactic (between galaxies) *space*: unimaginable distances.

God keeps each heavenly body and combinations of bodies protected from each other and other harm by creating for each its orbit in a vast universe, providing gravitational forces, etc. Modern science and technology have given us a better knowledge of how the earth, its atmosphere, and life on it are protected.

Very high energy radiation from the sun converts some atmospheric oxygen to ozone. The upper layer of the stratosphere, 15 miles above the ground, has about six parts of ozone per million parts of air. This ozone shields the earth from the sun's ultraviolet rays. They cause sunburn; excessive exposure causes skin cancer.

X-rays are produced in space by the sun, other stars, pulsars, and certain other heavenly bodies. Most of these X-rays are absorbed by the atmosphere before they reach the earth. An overdose of X-rays may produce in humans skin burns, cancer, reduction of the blood supply, and cause other serious conditions; it can destroy the tissues of living creatures.

Meteoroids are pieces of metallic or stony matter, belonging to the solar system, which enter the earth's atmosphere from space; before burning up, they are called meteorites; and those that burn are called meteors, or falling or shooting stars. The thin air of the upper atmosphere begins to heat a meteoroid, causing it to glow and create a trail of hot gases. Friction of the denser atmosphere heats it and the air around to about 4000 °F, and it usually breaks and burns up at altitudes of 30-50 miles. Scientists estimate that nearly 200 million visible meteors occur daily in the atmosphere; most of them are small like a grain of sand. However, the Tunguska meteorite that crashed into the earth in Siberia in 1908 had an estimated weight of a few hundred tons. A meteorite that exploded over the Sikhote-Alin Mountains in Siberia in 1947 made more than 200 craters in the earth. In the 1950s scientists discovered five large meteorite craters in Canada; the largest made a 400-mile wide depression, and the others have 1½ to about 8 miles wide craters. The friction of air in the atmospheric layers, their temperatures, etc., cause most meteoroids to burn up as meteors. This protects the earth and its inhabitants from fire and destruction.

Conclusion
Modern science shows us that the heavenly bodies in the solar system and space systems beyond are kept in their own orbits and in relative security from foreign intrusions by their own gravitational fields and other determinants.

The variety of temperatures and gases in the air, its densities and resistance, and other characteristics of the atmospheric layers provide a shield for the earth, and life on it, protecting it from many hazards. Modern science has provided us explanations of the Qur'anic verses cited above.

Notes

S.v., "Air", "Meteor", "Ozone", "Sun", "X-Rays", *The World Book Encyclopedia*, 1981.

23. Sun's and Earth's Magnetic Fields

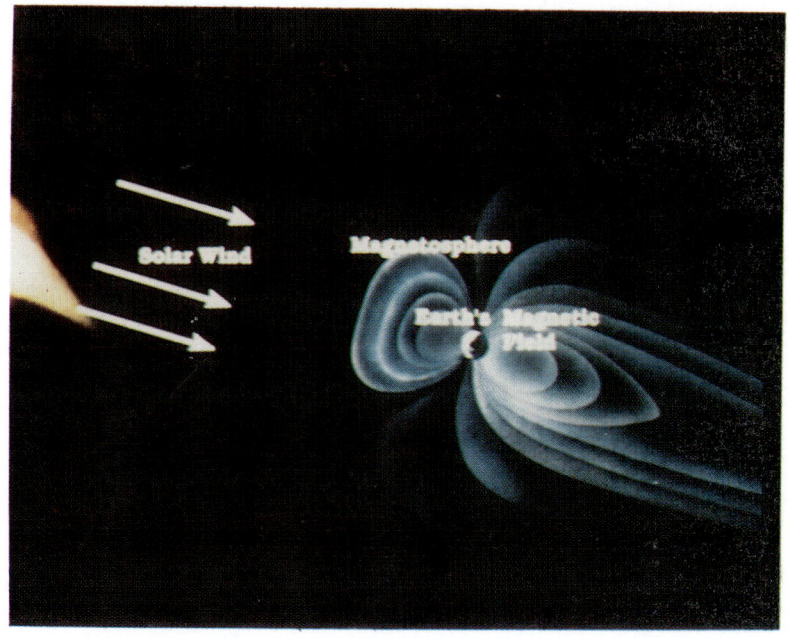

And He decreed that it [the sky] become seven [many] heavens in two days [aeons], and imparted to each heaven its function. And He adorned the sky nearest to the earth with lights, and made them well-protected. Such is the determination of the Almighty, the All-knowing. **(Qur'an 41:12)**

The sun sends out charged particles called the solar wind at speeds of about a million miles per hour. However, the earth's upper atmosphere is dominated by magnetic fields and electric currents which form a bubble around it that protects the planet from these particles. When the solar wind encouters this upper atmosphere, this mingling of matter, energy, and magnetism transfers massive amounts of energy from the sun to Earth.

24. The Aurora

Behold, We have adorned the sky nearest to the earth with the beauty of stars, and made them well-protected from every rebellious, satanic force. **(Qur'an 37:6-7)**

The sun's atmosphere, which is blown off into space as the solar wind, is composed of charged particles, protons and electrons. A strong magnetic field around the earth deflects and concentrates them at Earth's magnetic poles. They collide with Earth's molecules of oxygen and nitrogen, and produce red, green and blue lights called the auroras. The auroral displays occur 70 miles or more above the earth's surface in its upper atmosphere, and can be seen at high latitudes. Thus magnetic fields and Earth's atmosphere protect Earth from the sun's harmful particles. ".. O God! Owner of sovereignty!...In Your hand is the good. Verily, You are able to do all things." (Qur'an 3:26)

25. Earth's Atmosphere: Ultraviolet Image of Tropical Arcs

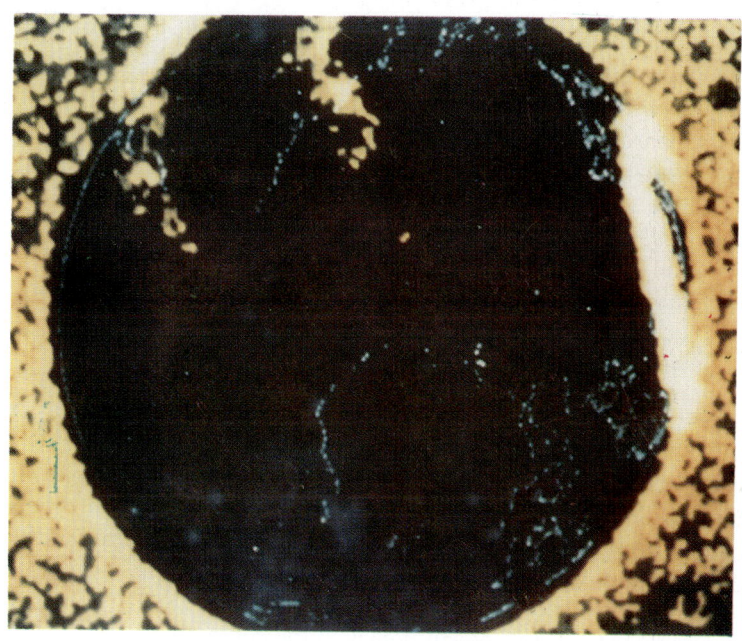

And, indeed, We set up in the sky planetary bodies, and endowed them with beauty for the observers. And We have protected them from every satanic force accursed so that anyone who seeks to hear by stealth is pursued by a clear flame. **(Qur'an 15:16-18)**

Earth's upper atmosphere is thought to be an envelope of gases and magnetic fields which absorb radiation and deflect harmful particles from space. Reactions between these gases, ions, and magnetic fields create a protective cocoon around the earth without which life as we know it cannot exist. It is feared that pollutants that enter the atmosphere may change these reactions. Instruments can see the effects of such activities. This view of Earth showing glowing oxygen atoms over the tropics and around the polar region was photographed by an instrument that collected ultraviolet light these atoms emit.

26-29. Stratospheric Air Temperatures & Pressures, Four Altitudes

The Most Gracious! He has taught the Qur'an. He has created man. He has taught him the means to articulate thought and speech. The sun and the moon are [orbiting] according to a reckoning. And the planetary bodies and trees do prostrate, and the sky has He raised high, and He has set up the balance, so that you shall not transgress the balance. And you should establish the balance with equity, and should not diminish (or cause loss in) the balance. And He has designed Earth for living creatures, wherein are fruit and sheathed palm trees, and grain growing on stalks, and sweet-smelling plants. Then which of the bounties of your Sustainer will you two disavow?
(Qur'an 55:1-13)

NASA's Nimbus satellite program, Limb Infrared Monitor of the Stratosphere, LIMS, detects heat radiating from Earth as infrared radiation and records temperatures which are depicted in different colors. The scale starts with the lowest at 175 degrees K in dark blue, and moves up to the maximum at 295 K in white. All air temperature measurements were made during February 21-25, 1979, over the Northern Hemisphere. North Pole is in the center of all 4 photos. The stratosphere absorbs the strongest rays of the sun, and shields Earth like an umbrella to prevent its biosphere from getting too hot. This shield and protective blanket, which wraps around it, is the ozone in the stratosphere. Mankind should maintain the environmental "balance" which God has designed for Earth, and observe the "balance" He has ordained in ethics and values in science, technology, and development.

26. Stratosphere: At 22 Miles Altitude

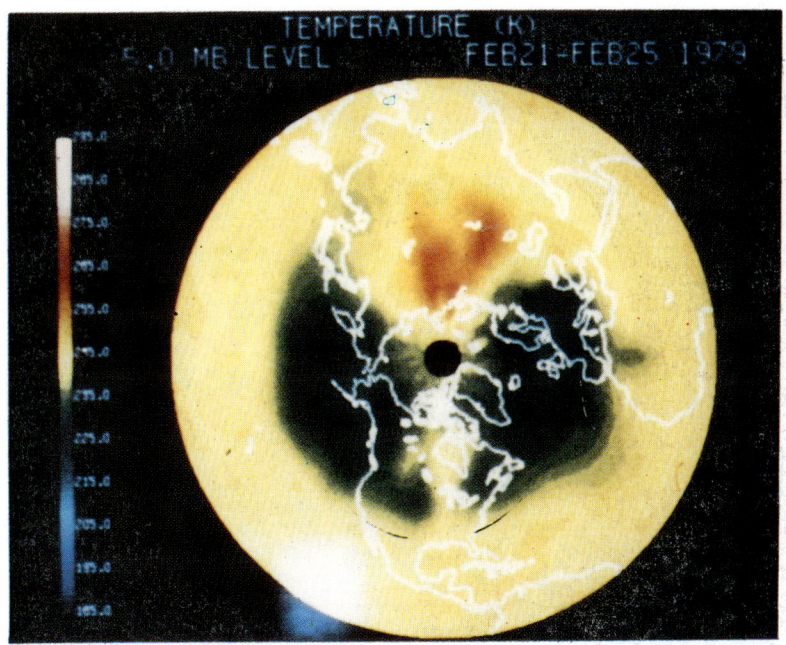

Air Temperatures at 22 Miles Altitude, 5 MB Pressure. Near the top of the stratosphere, 22 miles above Earth, the air is very thin with only 5 MB (millibars) air pressure, and the temperatures are at their highest.

27. Stratosphere: At 19 Miles Altitude

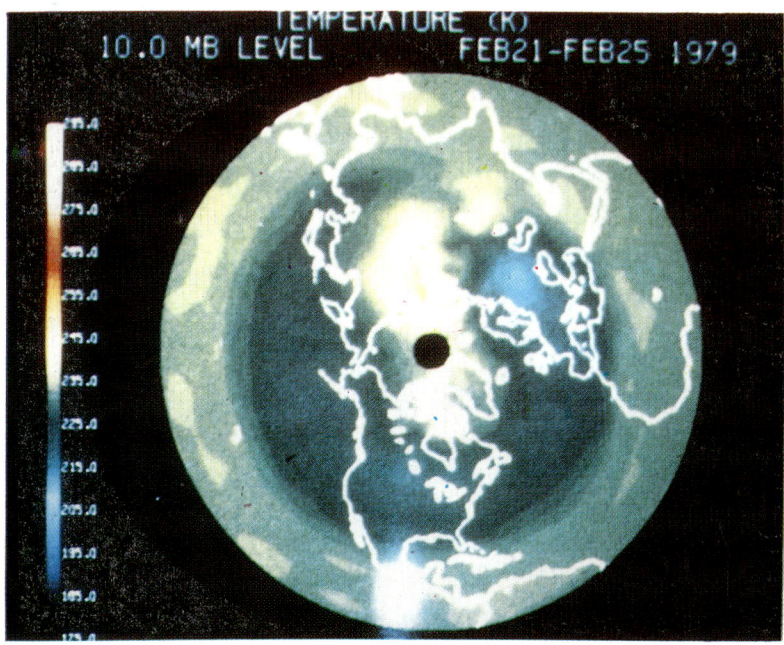

Air Temperatures at 19 Miles Altitude, 10 MB Pressure. At 19 miles above Earth, air pressure is twice as great at 10 MB. The temperatures have gone down, showing more areas of blue, because the air does not absorb much radiation from the sun.

28. Stratosphere: At 15 Miles Altitude

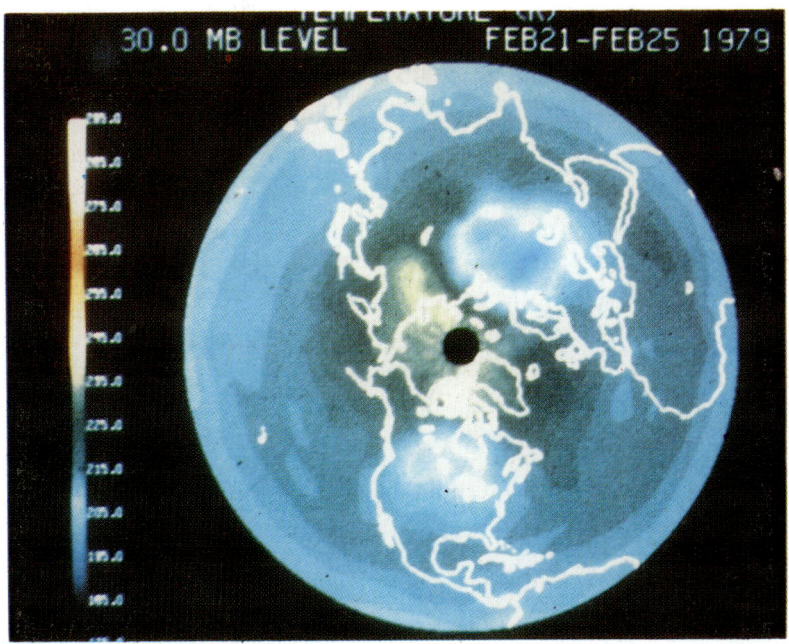

Air Temperatures at 15 Miles Altitude, 30 MB Pressure. At 15 miles altitude, with more air in the atmosphere, air pressure has risen to 30 MB. The temperatures are mostly cool, and are nearly 235 degrees K at the coolest around the North Pole.

29. Stratosphere: At 10 Miles Altitude

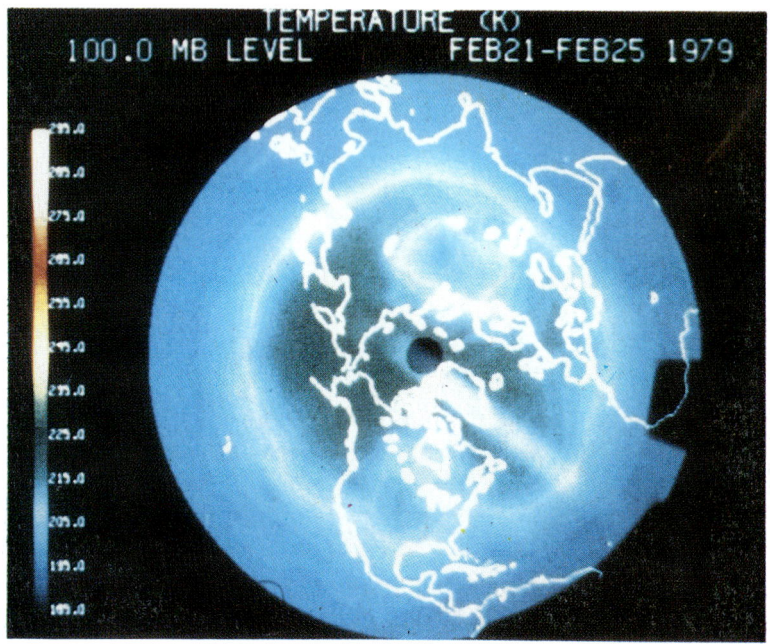

Air Temperatures at 10 Miles Altitude, 100MB Pressure. At 10 miles above Earth, near the bottom of the stratosphere, the air pressure is the highest for this layer at 100 MB. The overall temperatures are very cool. These pictures indicate that temperatures increase as we travel up through the stratosphere. *...That is the determination of the Mighty, the Wise. (Qur'an 36:38)*

30. Ozone Hole: Stratospheric Ozone Concentration, 1979-1990

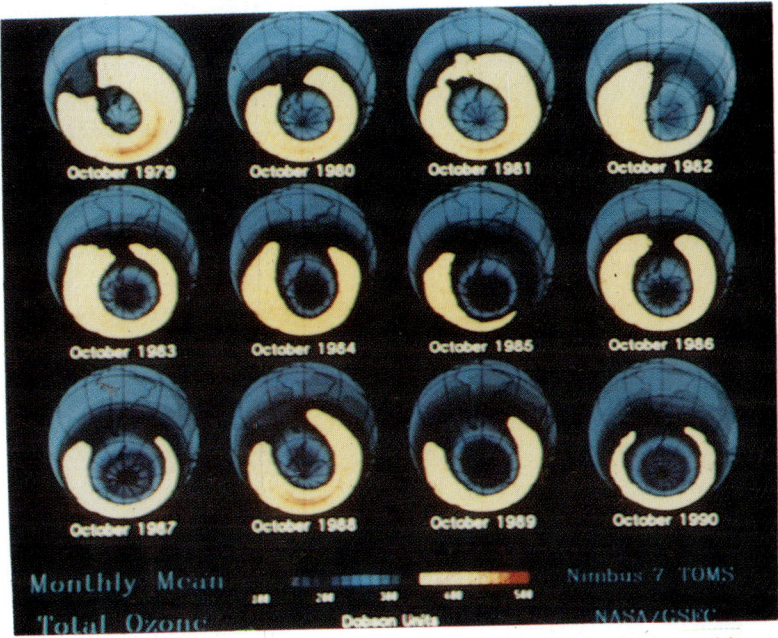

And of mankind is he whose conversation on the life of this world may please thee, and he calls God to witness as to that which is in his heart; and he is exceedingly skillful in argument. And when he turns away, he strives on the earth to spread corruption therein, and destroy tilth and progeny [e.g., environmental life support systems]; and God loves not mischief. **(Qur'an 2:204-5)**

These 12 pictures show changes in stratospheric ozone concentration from 1979 and 1990. Red and yellow depict the greatest ozone concentration; the size of their areas decreased over the South Pole. The purple over the polar region shows areas with the lowest concentration. Ozone is essential to protect human, plant and animal life from excessive ultraviolet radiation, and to provide energy for other chemical reactions in the stratosphere. Man's activities, in the name of progress and development for happiness, are threatening the basis of life on Earth by disturbing, if not destroying, the stability of the ozone layer. *...Would you exchange that wherein there is benefit, with that which is lower?...* **(Qur'an 2:61)**

31-34. Stratospheric Ozone Variation: 4 Days, 1979, at 19 miles

And We have set up the sky as a canopy well-protected. And yet from its signs they turn away stubbornly. **(Qur'an 21:32)**

NASA's instrument, Limb Infrared Monitor of Stratosphere, LIMS, recorded the distribution of atmospheric ozone on four different days. These four pictures look at the Northern Hemisphere around the North Pole at an altitude of about 19 miles above Earth, and 10.0 MB air pressure. On a scale from zero to 12.0, the least concentration of ozone is shown in blue, and the highest in red. Ozone is a very small percentage of Earth's atmosphere. Ozone absorbs the ultraviolet radiation from the sun which is the prime cause of sunburn and skin cancer.

31. Ozone Concentration,
Day #1: Feb. 6, 1979

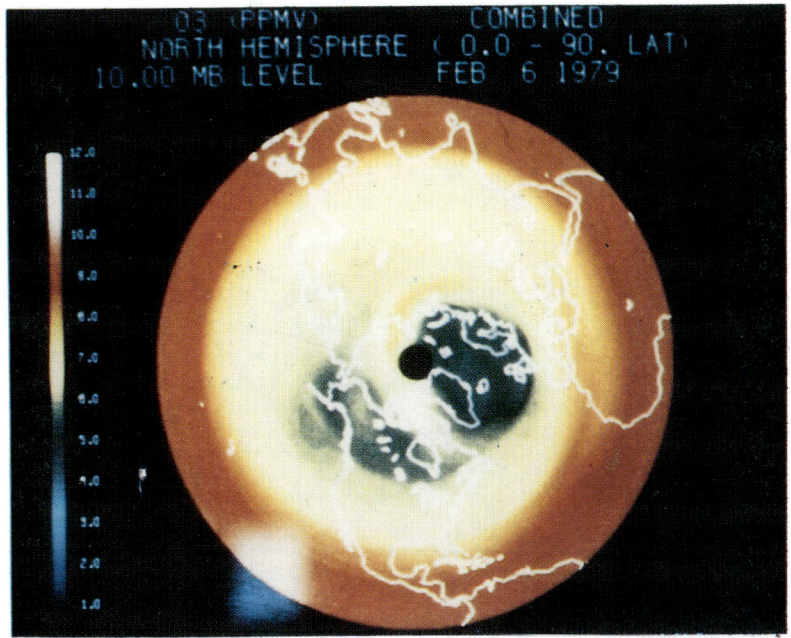

The first photo of February 6 shows a large area near the North Pole with low levels of ozone concentration, depicted in shades of blue.

32. Ozone Concentration, Day #2: Feb. 16, 1979

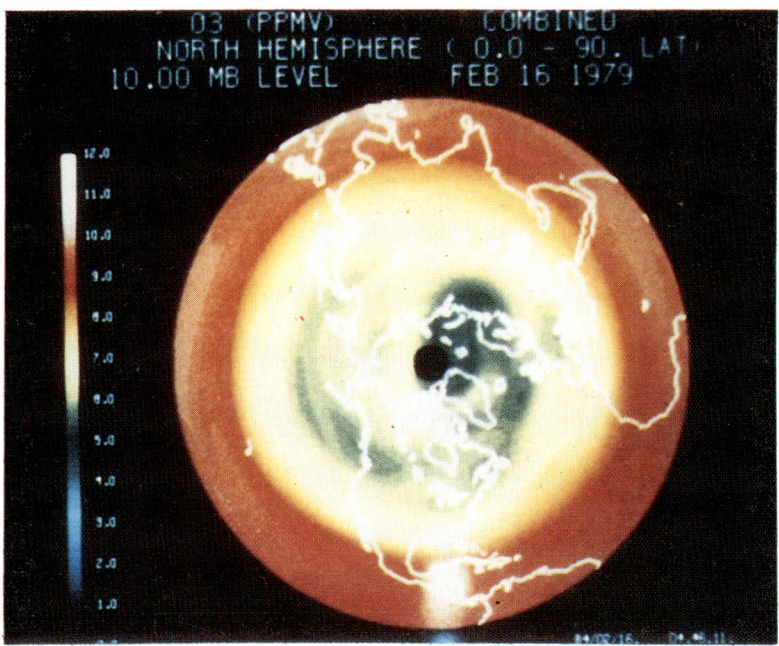

The February 16 photo shows that the ozone had moved around and the areas of concentration had changed. The area from which ozone concentrations have disappeared is not well protected from the sun's harmful radiation.

33. Ozone Concentration,
Day # 3: Feb. 23, 1979

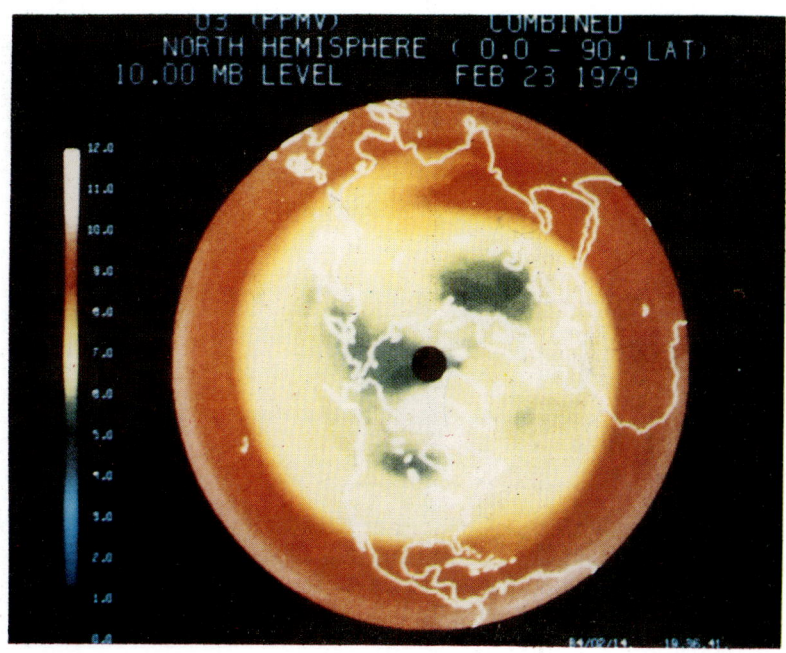

By February 23, the areas and concentration of ozone continued to shift and change. The stratosphere contains 90% of the ozone in our air. Some areas in this picture in shades of blue continued to have low ozone concentrations.

34. Ozone Concentration,
Day # 4: March 1, 1979

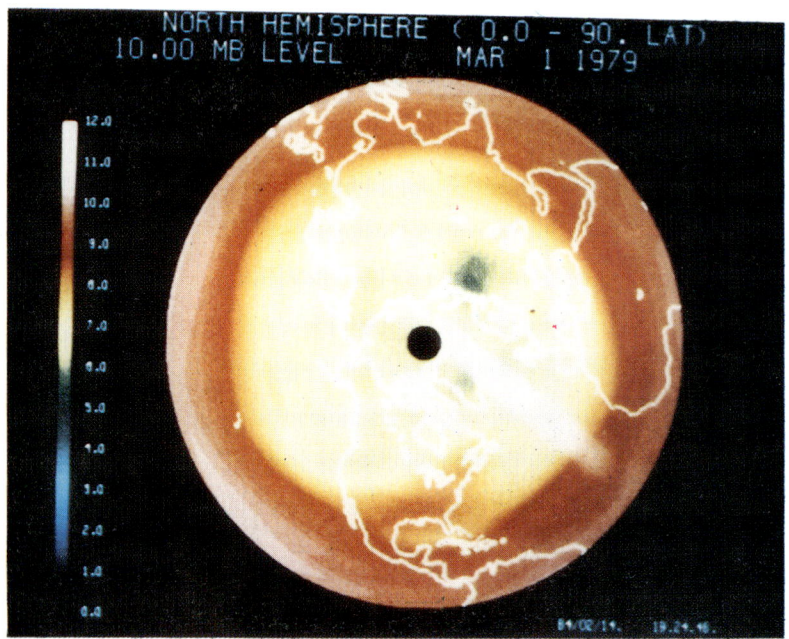

The mostly yellow and red color indicates the increase in ozone concentration by the 1st of March. Ozone shelters plant and animal life also from the sun's ultraviolet radiation.

CHAPTER 13

Light and Vision[1]

Introduction

This chapter discusses verses from the Qur'an concerning the characteristics of light and darkness; differentiation between self-emitting and other bodies, and their effect on human vision; and man's vision, and his reactions, as he ascends into space. The key Qur'anic words are: light (*nur*); darknesses (*zulumat*); to shine, glitter, illumine, or illumination (v. *ada'a*, n. *diya'un*) 'to see', watch, gain enlightenment, and the sight, vision (n. *al-basaru*); blind (n. *'umyun*)

The Qur'an on Light and Darknesses, and Changes in Vision as Man Ascends into Sky.

All praise is due to God, who has created the heavens and the earth, and brought into being the darknesses and light; and yet, those who are bent on Denying regard other powers as their Sustainer's equals! (6:1, Asad n 1)

Their similitude is that of a people who kindle a fire: but as soon as it has illumined all around them, God takes away their light, and leaves them in darknesses, wherein they can not see; deaf, dumb, blind — and they can not turn back. (2:17-18)

Yet even had We opened to them a gateway to heaven, and they had ascended, on and on, in it, they would surely have said: 'Indeed, our sights are spellbound (lit., intoxicated, sukkirat)! Nay, we are a people bewitched! (15:14-15, n 14)

Summary and Explanation

God has created light and darknesses; they are not equal (Qur'an 13:16; 35:20). The sun is a self-emitting source of light; the moon gives reflected light as discussed in Chapter 9 (Qur'an 10:5;' 25:61; 71:16). The famous verse, "God is the light of the heavens and the earth" (24:35), gives a few similitudes on light. It mentions different sources, fuels, and containers of light, and a non-earthly "tree" whose "oil" gives "illumination" though "no fire has touched it." What, then, is light? What are its different kinds, and their properties? How does light behave in contact with various materials? What is the relation between light, human eyes, and man's belief systems?

There are 23 verses in which "darknesses" are mentioned in the plural form, and none with darkness in the singular noun form. What is the significance of this in the scientific context? What is darkness, and how is it created or brought about?

Verse 2:17 describes a phenomenon. A fire is kindled;

its light is scattered all around, and one sees objects. When no light is produced from the burning source; man can not see objects around him. How are the sensations of sight and darkness produced? What are the roles of the human eye and light in vision?

The last verses present a phenomenon that we know only recently after the first flights in space were undertaken. It was beyond the capabilities of man's theoretical and experimental sciences, and his experiences, for 1400 years since this verse was revealed to Prophet Muhammad. As man continues to ascend into space, how do the earth, the atmosphere and environment around him, and the distant heavenly objects and space look? How are the changing sights from space interpreted by those who deny or accept God?

Modern Knowledge of the Sources and Nature of Light
What are light and "darknesses" in modern science? Light, or visible light, is a tiny part of radiant energy that we can see. Radiant energy which is not visible to man includes the infrared, ultraviolet, and X rays, and radio waves; we are "blind" to them. The natural (sun) and artificial (candles) sources of light give off their own light; most things do not, but we see them because light travels from a source to them and then to our eyes.

Scientists believe that light comes from atoms of every element. An atom can absorb energy when it is "excited," for example, by burning; when it releases energy, light is produced. Atoms absorb and release energy in tiny bundles called photons. Light of different colors is produced when the source emits different amounts of energy. Red light is produced by photons with the least energy, and blue light by the most energetic photons. White light, consisting of all seven colors (red, orange, yellow, green, blue, indigo, and violet) is a mixture of photons of different levels of energy. Two theories were developed about the nature of light. One theory describes light as an emission of particles; the other states that light travels by wave motion. The quantum theory explains that both are true. Under certain conditions light behaves like a series of particles, and in other conditions it behaves like an electromagnetic wave. Certain interactions between light and matter, such as the photoelectric effect, demonstrate the particle-like nature of light.

Where light travels in wave motion, it has been found that the wave vibrates at right angles to the direction of travel. Light waves have an amplitude (strength) and a wave length (the distance at any point between two consecutive waves). Wave frequency is the number of waves passing any point per second. The amplitude determines the intensity, or brightness, of light. The electromagnetic spectrum is a chart that has arranged these waves according to their frequencies and wave lengths. "Visible light" has wave lengths from about 4000 to 7000 angstroms. An angstrom is about 0.0000001 millimeter. The whole spectrum ranges from the short gamma rays of 0.00000000001 mm (1/10,000 angstrom) or less, to the long radio waves of many miles. Thus the "visible spectrum" of electromagnetic waves that our eyes can see is a very tiny part of the whole spectrum. At either ends are vast darknesses, or areas of man's blindness.

Spectrum analysis is the study of the spectrum from different sources of light. When sunlight is made to pass through a prism, the wave lengths spread out and form a continuous spectrum of the seven colors of our visible spectrum. Sunlight has all the wave lengths of visible light. However, light from other sources may not have all the wave lengths of a continuous spectrum; there may be "dark gaps" or missing colors in the spectrum.

Optics (The Study of Light):
When a ray of light strikes an object, it may be reflected (thrown back), refracted (pass into it, and bend), absorbed by the object, or a combination of these may happen. Light is scattered in all directions when it strikes particles of matter such as those in the atmosphere. The amount and distribution of scattering (a kind of reflection) depends on the particle size, the wave length of light, etc. When two light waves come together, and the peak of one comes together with the trough (low point) of another, this interference cancels the light waves, leaving darkness. Polarization occurs when the electric and magnetic fields of photons in a beam of light line up in the same direction. A polaroid material lets only photons with fields in one direction pass through it; thus polarized sunglasses block the polarized part of the light, and reduce the glare or create "darkness."

The Human Eye, and Vision (or How we See):
The human eye does not actually see objects; it sees the light reflected by the objects. The parts of the eye include the cornea, which consists of tough tissues at the outer

layer of the eyeball; it lets in light rays. Behind it is the iris containing melanin which absorbs strong light that might otherwise dazzle the eye and cause blurred vision. The pupil, an adjustable opening in the iris, regulates the amount of light entering the eye. The crystalline lens, behind the iris, is a flexible structure with cells called rods and cones; they absorb light rays and change them into electrical signals. The optic nerve, which are nerve fibers attached to the rods and cones, carries electrical signals from the retina to the brain which interprets them as visual images.

Light rays entering the eye must come to a point on the retina to form a clear visual image. The cornea and lens are the focusing parts of the eye; they must refract the rays to make them come together on the retina and form the image on it. The lens provides the power to focus on distant or near objects, for less or more refraction, by becoming rounder and thicker. Defects and diseases of the eye interfere with the ability to focus images clearly and register color. Depending on the nature of the defect, the resulting image will be distorted to the point of being nonexistent (blindness); these may be called levels of "darknesses" or blindness.

Conclusions

Some verses of the Qur'an introduce the subjects of light, eyes, vision, etc. as creations of God. Words understandable in all ages by the common man are used in these verses; they also raise questions, and provide God's "signs" or "messages" (ayat) as a "guidance" about some scientific facts and ethical truths.

The verse 2:17 about a fire kindled allows us, through scientific knowledge, to differentiate between light from its "sources" and the light reflected and scattered from dark objects all around the source. Vision of the surrounding objects is lost, plunging one into various levels of darkness or blindness in relation to those objects, when the source of light is extinguished. Thus a distinction is made between a self-emitting source of light and, on the other hand, dark bodies which can only reflect light. Some scientific explanations of "darknesses" were given above by pointing out the roles of the human eye and light in vision.

Astronauts and pictures have described the sights of earth and space since space flights began in 1961. From above the earth's atmosphere, the sky does not have an azure color; that appearance from the earth is due to absorption of the sun's light in the layers of atmosphere, and scattering of light by the atmospheric particles. Man in space observes a black sky below towards the earth, like the black color of interstellar space, though the sun is shining and the stars are visible; and the earth appears surrounded by a bluish halo. The sky, viewed from the moon too, looks black during the day. This is because space does not have, like the earth's atmosphere, particles of matter to scatter sunlight, producing on the eye the familiar image of a blue sky. As mentioned in the Qur'an, those who have no knowledge of these scientific explanations, would doubt their sight and senses if they were transported into upper atmosphere and space.

Notes

[1] The earlier revealed Books of God, like the Torah and the Gospel (Qur'an 5:44, 46), were also a light (*nur*). The Qur'an, "The Book," and its messages or verses (*ayat*), are repeatedly referred to as the light which brings mankind from the darknesses into light (Qur'an 5:15; 7:157; 14:1, 5; 39:22; 57:9; 64:8; etc.). However, this chapter deals with light mostly as an Islamic science of physics, including optics, the physiology of the human eye, and vision.

S.v. "Eye", "Light", "Space Travel", *World Book Encyclopedia*, 1984.

35. Atmospheric Pollutants, West Africa

Do you not see how God raises clouds, then gathers them, then makes them layers, then you see rain come from between them. He sends from the sky mountainous masses wherein is hail, and smites with it whom He will and averts from it whom He will. The flash of His lightning nearly snatches away the sight.
(Qur'an 24:43)

These clouds colored by oblique sunlight highlight their gases and particles; they can have a beneficial or harmful impact on climate, environment, and health. The bronze hue is due to particles of a dust storm. Precipitation clouds are produced when water vapor molecules coalesce around dust particles. Industrial pollutants yield shades of blue and mauve, and volcanic ash clouds are depicted in red glow. Winds take clouds far. This picture was taken over the Atlantic, hundreds of miles from the source of a West African dust storm.

36. Agricultural Burning, Madagascar

It is He who shows you the lightning, a fear and hope, and raises the heavy clouds. And thunder hymns His praise and the angels in awe of Him. And He sends the thunderbolts and strikes with them whom He will. Yet they dispute about God, and He is strong in contriving that wherein is wisdom. **(Qur'an 13:12 n29)**

The extensive smoke clouds drifting across Lake Nayasa, joining with more produced in Tanzania, obscure astronauts' view of the earth. Point sources of smoke are discernible. Such pictures show that clouds of smoke travel far from their source, cover hundreds of square miles, and pollute vast areas of the lower atmosphere. Industrial pollutants rained out produce the harmful acid rain. The "heavy clouds" may also be those burdened with agricultural and industrial pollutants besides the water-bearing ones.

37. Gypsy Moth Defoliation, Harrisburg, Pennsylvania, U.S.A.

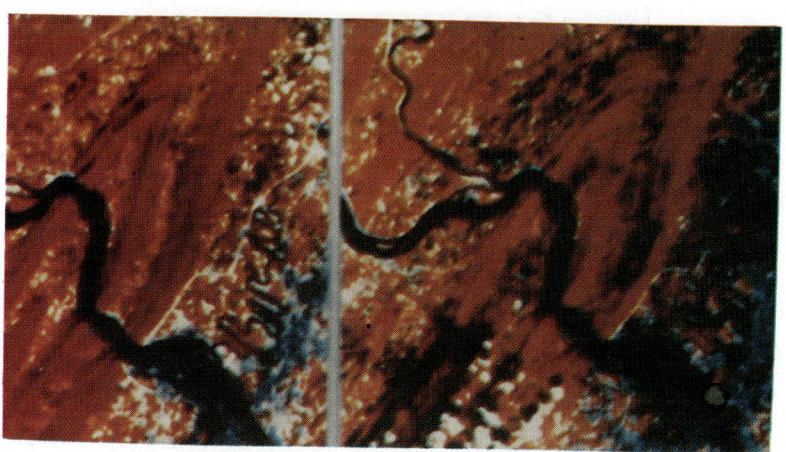

Among His signs is the creation of the heavens and the earth, and of whatever living creatures he has dispersed in both of them. And He is able to gather them when He will. And whatever calamity strikes you, it is what your right hands have earned, and He forgives much. **(Qur'an 42:29f)**

These Landsat sub-images of the Harrisburg area show the forest canopy in 1976 before (left), and in 1977 after defoliation by the Gypsy Moth caterpillar. Defoliation is represented by the brownish discoloration along the ridges of the images.

38. Wildland Fires, 1988, Yellowstone National Park, U.S.A.

...Say: All is from God. What, then, is amiss with these people that they come not near to understand a saying? Whatever good befalls you is from God, and whatever bad befalls you is from yourself. And We have sent thee [O Muhammad] *as a messenger unto mankind, and God is sufficient as witness.*
(Qur'an 4:78f)

This image of the Yellowstone Park shows the early stages of the wildland fires, 1988. The burned vegetation is shown in tones of red and purple. The white and light blue represent smoke from active fires. The healthy vegetation is green, and the darker green are the dense timber stands. As God's vicegerents on earth, people must prevent or mitigate fires even due to natural causes through Islamic ethical and scientific forest management.

CHAPTER 14

Lightning: Benefits and Harm

Introduction

This chapter presents all the five Qur'anic verses on lightning. The phenomenon, and its benefits and hazards are discussed using modern atmospheric and other geophysical sciences. The key words and concepts under discussion include: lightning *(al-barq)* as a scientific phenomenon, and its technological, psychological (or spiritual), and socioeconomic effects; and its potential impact on sight (pl., *al-absar*).

The Qur'an on Lightning

Or [the similitude is] *of a violent cloudburst in the sky, wherein are darknesses and thunder and lightning. They put their fingers into their ears, to keep out the peals of thunder, in terror of death. But God encompasses the Deniers.*

The lightning well-nigh takes away their sight; whenever it illuminates for them, they advance therein, and whenever darkness falls around them, they stand still. And if God so willed, He could take away their hearing and their sight; for, verily, God has the power to will anything. (2:19-20, Asad n12)

He it is who displays before you the lightning, to give rise to fear and hope, and calls heavy clouds into being. (13:12, n27)

Do you not see that it is God who causes the clouds to move onward, then joins them together, then piles them up in masses, until you can see the rain come forth from their midst? And He it is who sends down from the sky mountainous masses [of clouds] charged with hail, striking therewith whomever He wills; the flash of His lightning well-nigh takes away the sight! (24:43)

And among His signs [ayat] *is this: He displays before you the lightning, giving rise to fear and hope, and sends down water from the sky, giving life thereby to the earth after it had been lifeless: in this, behold, there are messages* (ayat) *indeed for people who use reason!* (30: 24)

Summary and Explanation

The verses above associate lightning with heavy clouds, *(al-sihab al-thiqal)* thunder *(al-ra'd)*, and "violent" cloudburst, *(sayyibun)*. The latter is associated with a root verb *asaba*, which means to strike, assail, inflict, etc. *Asaba* and *sayyibun* connote a strong or forceful action; thus God creates a kind of cloud which produces lightning and thunder. The lightning more or less takes away sight, and can create in certain kinds of people an abnormal fear of death. If God so willed, though He normally does not, He can cause loss of sight by the intensity of lightning. People can walk in the short-lived illumination produced by it. But the ensuing darkness takes away all sense of sight; the eye is unable to adjust to the quick changes, and people are "blinded" temporarily. They are obliged to stand still. Lightning is a source of both fear and hope. A hope that is often realized is heavy precipitation. It revives the earth that was dead in terms of biological activities and productivity.

Some of the questions we may ask are: What is lightning, how is it produced, and what are its beneficial and harmful effects? Is lightning inherently bad and harmful, that we should wish (or "pray") that it does not occur at all, and is it preventable? Or does it have elements of both "fear" and "hope"? How can we realize this "hope" of benefits, and reduce the "fear" of harm and damage caused by lightning? How and when does lightning take away sight, temporarily or permanently? What is the meaning of the oft-repeated concept in the Qur'an that such phenomena are the "signs" (*ayat*) of God? What are the "signs of God" in lightning that rational or educated people can know?

Pre-Qur'anic and Modern Scientific Views on Lighting

In Western cultures, the Greeks and Romans looked upon lightning as a weapon of their gods. People and places struck by lightning were considered cursed in some African societies. Christians in Europe and America believed, at least until the 1700s, that ringing church bells kept away lightning. Similarly, anthropologists could cite psuedo-Islamic beliefs and practices of Muslims, and myths and superstitions in other cultures, about lightning. These are un-Islamic and "unscientific."

The lightning we see is a giant spark of electricity between a cloud and the earth. It consists of electrical strokes or discharges. What is seen as a bright light is the return stroke; it travels at about the speed of light which is 186,282 miles per second. These strokes may discharge about 100 million volts of electricity; each stroke may be 15 million volts; they may heat the air in their way to over 60,000 degrees F. The air heated thus expands quickly; it produces a pressure wave called thunder.

The human being's adaptation to light and darkness occurs in the pupil and, more important, the retina. The pupil may become small like a pinhead to prevent the eye from being damaged or dazzled by too much light. In the retina light rays are absorbed by pigments in the rods and cones (the light-sensitive cells). Light-sensitive chemicals in the rods and cones react to specific wave lengths of light and trigger nerve impulses to the brain.

The retina contains ten to fifteen times more rods than cones. The rods do not detect line, point or color; they perceive the light and dark tones in an image, and can distinguish outlines of objects in nearly complete darkness. Rods detect images in darkness because they contain a pigment called visual purple, or rhodopsin. When exposed to light visual purple undergoes a chemical change in which it loses its color, and this causes the rods to lose their sensitivity to light and thus escape harm from too much brightness. But before the eye can see in the dark, the visual purple must be restored, a process which requires vitamin A. It is difficult at first to see in dim light because the rhodopsin was bleached out by exposure to bright light. Depending on how much it was bleached, it takes 10 to 30 minutes for rhodospin to be renewed. Thus lightning can plunge one into darkness, or a kind of temporary blindness.

How do meteorologists explain the occurrence of lightning? It is associated with cumulonimbus clouds (thunderclouds). Matter is made up of atoms which may become charged positive or negative by losing or gaining electrons. Lightning is the spark of electric current resulting from the movement of charged particles within a cumulonimbus cloud, between such a cloud and the ground, etc. Thus lightning could be intracloud, cloud-to-air, cloud-to-cloud, cloud-to-ground, etc. depending on the direction in which the charges first begin to flow.

People can avoid getting struck by lightning by taking safety measures during thunderstorms. Lightning strikes the earth nearly 100 times a year. Lightning rods (metal poles) attached to building tops, and wired to a ground rod buried 10 feet or more in moist earth, protects from lightning. They are not needed in cities if there is much metal used in buildings that stand close together.

Air contains about 78% nitrogen and 21% oxygen. Protoplasm is the living material in all animal tissues and plants. Nitrogen is an important part of the protein molecules in protoplasm. Lightning causes nitrogen and oxygen in the air to form nitrogen oxides; they form nitric acid with water which is carried to the earth in rainwater. Some of the nitric acid used by plants to manufacture their protein comes from atmospheric rainwater. Thus lightning plays a part in the nitrogen cycle: God's way to "naturally" circulate nitrogen among the atmosphere, soil, water, plants and animals of the earth. The pollution caused by nitrogen compounds in air, water, and soil is the work of man; we produce them through combustion of gasoline, manufacture them as nitrogen fertilizers, etc., and misuse them through our careless technology.

Conclusions

The generalized "fear" and "hope" mentioned in the Qur'anic verses are directly related to lightning through fire, death, losses, natural soil fertility and agricultural productivity through nitrification, etc. Man's understanding and application of these *ayat* of God brings direct benefits and avoidance of harm; the *kafirun* (literally, the Ingrates, or those who Deny) are the people who do not get these benefits or avoid damages due to their ignorance and the misuse of the sciences and technology.

The basic Qur'anic idea is that lightning, and other hydro-meteorological variables and phenomena are among the "signs" or "messages" of God. This means that the creation of certain clouds, the generation of lightning and thunder, the consequent precipitation with "normal" or "extreme" floods, the many losses and benefits, are all subject to God's laws of the sciences of nature and human behaviour. The "laws" governing these geophysical sciences, like meteorology and hydrology, are also God's determination (*taqdir*, Qur'an 6:96; 13:8; 25:2; 36:38; etc.). God made these physical laws in the very nature of the earth and heavens. It is man's duty to know and apply these *ayat* or laws of God. Man must adopt appropriate technological and social means so as to gain the benefits and avoid the harm of lightning.

The variables mentioned in these verses are hydro-meteorological parameters for certain functions or relationships. The dependent variables are God's "signs" (laws), clouds, lightning, thunder, precipitation, etc. The independent variables may be lightning or precipitation as a function of particular kinds of clouds, and the benefits and losses. Buildings and their occupants could be harmed by lightning; but they could avoid harm by using lightning rods to dissipate the electricity harmlessly into the ground.

The mountainous masses of clouds with darknesses mentioned in the above verses would describe the cumulus (piled-up) and nimbus (rain bearing) clouds; the latter are dark gray rain clouds. These clouds may rise to great heights while their bases are near the ground. A cumulonimbus cloud may extend to a height of 60,000 feet from very low altitudes. Since they are heaped-up piles of cloud, by reflecting and absorbing sunlight they create different layers of darkness along their height.

Lightning between a cloud and the atmosphere scatters electric energy in the air. Through His laws and purpose, if God were to dissipate this intensity of light and pressure closer to the earth, instead of in the upper atmosphere, people would be made blind and deaf. When lightning does strike the ground, it may cause fire, death, and damage.

Notes

S.v., "Lightning," "Lightning rod"; also "Air", "Cloud", "Nitrogen," and "Nitrogen Cycle", *World Book Encyclopedia,* 1984 and 1981.

39. Sediment-laden Drainage Basin, Betsiboka River, Madagascar

There was indeed a sign for Sheba in their homeland, two gardens on the right and left: 'Eat of the provision from your Sustainer and render thanks to Him. A good land, and a forgiving Sustainer!' But they turned away, so We sent on them the flooding of the dams and changed their two gardens into a couple of gardens bearing bitter fruit, the tamarisk and some lote-trees. **(Qur'an 34:15f)**

The Betsiboka flows for 525 km; nearly 130 km are navigable. The lower reaches, with red sediment in the picture, have extensive rice fields. Observations from space show that the tropical forest now does not exist since deforestation started in the 1960s. Yemen, known as the Kingdom of Sheba, was lost in the first millennium B.C., when sedimentation caused floods, destroying hydraulic structures, irrigated lands, and the nation.

40. Mouth of the Amazon River, Brazil

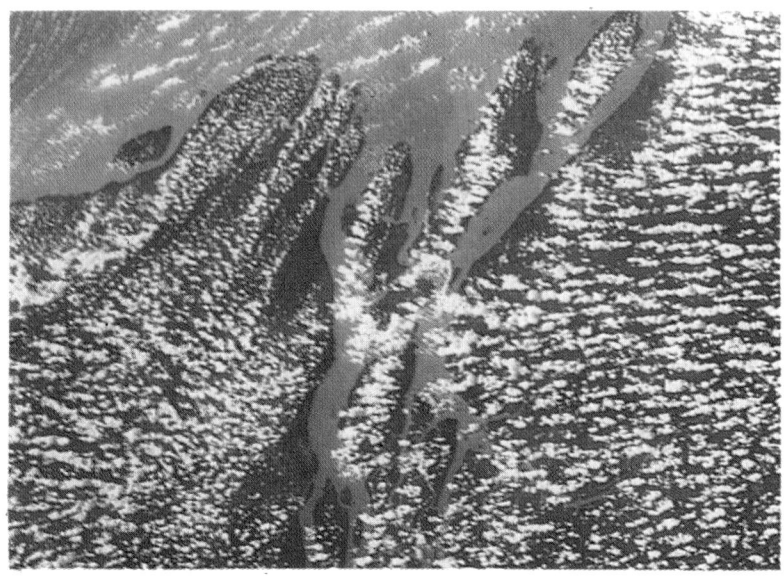

...And you all should be faithful in measurement and balance and do not diminish to people their things; and do not spread corruption on earth after it has been so well ordered. This is for your own good, if you would but believe. **(Qur'an 7:85)**

The Amazon River has deposited millions of cubic meters of sediment in the Atlantic Ocean. The sediment was the rich but thin layer of tropical topsoil of the Amazon Basin. The sediment plume from the river extends beyond the delta which was itself built of sediment deposits; the plume is driven northward by the Guyana Current. The land use policy of converting rain forest to agricultural land has aggravated erosion.

CHAPTER 15

Altitude Sickness

Introduction

Only one Qur'anic verse alludes to the physiological effects of ascending in "the sky." The Qur'anic key words and concepts include: heart, bosom (*sadar*); ascending (*yass"adu*); sky (*sama'*): punishment (*rijs*); restricted, narrow, hence difficult (*haraj*); constricted, straitened, hence troubled (*dayyiqa*); the people who seek admonition or remembrance (*qawmin yazzakkarun*) from God's signs (*ayat*).

The Qur'an on Attitude Sickness

So whomsoever God wills to guide, his bosom He opens wide towards Islam (lit., the surrender); *and whomsoever He wills to let go astray, his bossom He causes to be restricted and constricted as if he were ascending in the sky. It is thus that God inflicts punishment on those who do not believe. And this, thy Sustainer's way, is straight. Clearly, indeed, have We*

spelled out the signs for people who take admonition!
(6:125-26, Asad n 111)

Summary and Explanation

There are many verses in the Qur'an where the heart (*qalb*) and the bosom or chest (*sadar*) are referred to in the physical and metaphorical senses. In this verse, 6:125, the bosom is mentioned twice but with two different meanings. Here we are concerned with only the physical effects of ascending in "the sky." The heart develops problems as if it was getting closed and constricted.

The questions we may raise are: Does ascending in the sky mean both going up to higher altitudes as in mountain climbing, and ascending into upper atmospheric regions and space? Are the conditions described in the verse correct according to our modern sciences and experiences? What causes the effects described in the two adjectives, and how can we interpret them? What kinds of problems, or punishments, can be expected from such ascending? What are God's "signs" or laws concerning such ascending in relation to human physiology? Who are the "believers," and the people who remember or take admonition from these signs of God?

Modern Knowledge on Ascending to Higher Altitudes, and Effects on the Heart

The earth's atmosphere is an "ocean" of air which gets thinner as we rise up. Over 99% of the atmosphere lies below the thermosphere; it is the layer that begins about 50 miles above the earth. With less air, air pressure decreases with altitude. It is 14.7 lbs. per square inch at sea level, 10.2

at 10,000 feet elevation, 6.4 at 20,000 feet, and only 1.6 lbs per inch at 50,000 feet (about 9.5 miles) altitude.

Man needs oxygen and air pressure to survive. Most persons are accustomed to living under 5,000 feet. The Tibetans and Indians of Bolivia have adapted to high altitudes upto 17,000 feet; they do hard labor though newcomers may be panting for breath at each step. The amount of oxygen entering the blood stream decreases at higher altitudes because of reduced atmospheric pressure. If the oxygen content of blood drops below the body-needs, one gets "altitude sickness." This is characterized by shortness of breath, fatigue, headache, dizziness, nausea, and faulty judgement.

Anoxia is the lack of a normal supply of oxygen to body tissues, or their failure to utilize oxygen. Anoxic anoxia occurs when blood flowing in the lungs does not take in enough oxygen due to lack of oxygen in the air breathed, or diseases of the lungs and blood. This scarcity of oxygen occurs at 10,000 to 15,000 feet altitude, in poorly ventilated areas, etc. Healthy persons develop symptoms of anoxic anoxia when they breathe air with two-thirds or less the normal oxygen content. They may lose consciousness when they get one-half or less of needed oxygen; but life may be saved if oxygen is given immediately.

Conclusions

Prophet Muhammad, and the people in Arabia, could not know or anticipate the conditions and problems of even mountain climbing. Almost none of the world's famous peaks were climbed until the 1800s. The Arabian peninsula, even Africa and West Asia, do not have the higher mountains of the world. However, the pre-Qur'anic literatures of the East and the West gave prominence to mountains and the sky in their epics and myths. These were the "mythical places" of their gods, goddesses, demons, and dead souls. By contrast, Qur'anic references to ascending the sky are associated with knowable laws and experiences of physiology and the atmospheric sciences.

The Qur'anic verse points out the hazards of ascending in the sky. It describes the symptoms associated with the reduction of air, oxygen, and atmospheric pressure, and the effect on the function of the heart which slows down and stops with the diminishing supply of oxygen in the blood. The "believers" and "people who mind or take admonition" are those who understand the "signs" of God concerning the body's need for oxygen, the natural or man-made conditions of scarcity of oxygen at higher altitudes, and take measures to prevent and avoid the "punishment" for violation of God's laws. For example, they provide for supply of oxygen when they travel in the air or space, go mountaineering, work in mines, etc.

Note

S.v., "Air", "Altitude", "Sickness", "Anoxia", "Mountain", "Mountain Climbing", "Mythology", "Oxygen", *World Book Encyclopedia*, 1984

41. Manicouagan Impact Crater, Quebec, Canada

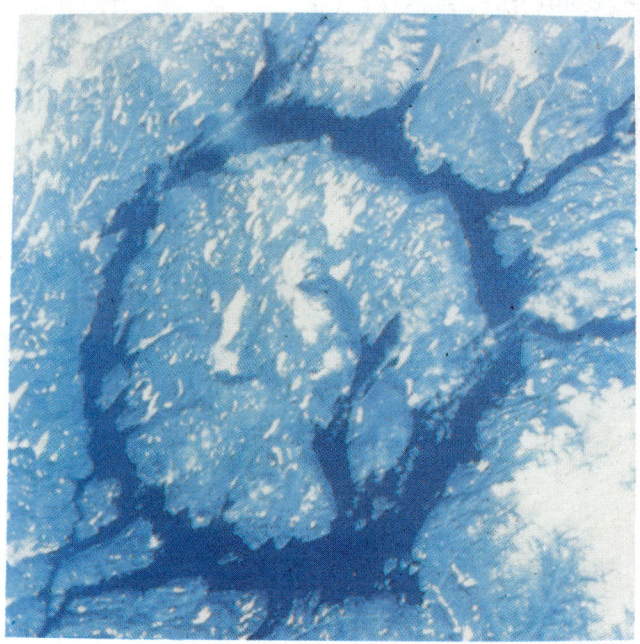

Have they, then, any diety other than God? Glorified be God from what they ascribe as partner (unto Him)! *And if they were to see a fragment from the sky falling down, they would say: A mass of clouds. Hence leave them till they meet their Day when they will be stricken with terror ; a Day in which their guile will avail them nothing, nor will they be helped.* **(Quran 52:43-46)**

Scientists believe that Manicouagan, 65 km diameter, is one of the largest terrestrial craters produced 200 million years ago. Perhaps an asteroidal impact caused extinctions of species such as dinosaurs at the end of the cretaceous period 60 million years ago. Such catastrophic collisions must have raised a dust cloud, obscured the sun, lowered temperatures, and produced environmental changes that were too drastic for some creatures to survive .

42. Richat Structure, Mauritania

Do you not see that God sends down water from the sky, whereby We bring forth fruits of diverse colors, and among the hills there are streaks of white and red of various shades and raven-black; and there are in men, and in crawling beasts, and in cattle too diverse hues. Indeed, among His servants only the scholars stand in awe of God. Verily, God is almighty, much-forgiving. **(Qur'an 35: 27-28)**

This circular feature in the Sahara desert, about 50 km diameter, has been a prominent geological attraction of space missions. It is perhaps a symmetrical uplift (circular anticline) laid bare by erosion. Paleozoic quartzites form the resistant beds outlining the structure. Some faults are conspicuous at lower right in the 4 o'clock position. Color variations are due to difference in mineral composition and weathering of the rock formations.

43. Aswan Dam and
Lake Nasser (1970), Egypt

He (God) sends down water from the sky so that valleys flow according to their measure, then the flood bears swelling foam; and from that which they smelt in the fire to make ornaments or useful goods likewise rises a foam. Thus God sets forth the truth and falsehood. Then, as for the foam, it passes away as scum; but what is of benefit to mankind abides on earth. Thus God coins the similitudes. **(Qur'an 13:17)**

The River Nile and Lake Nasser, the airstrip in 4 o'clock position from the Dam, and irrigated areas are seen against the desert landscape. The dendritic offshoots and backed up water reveal the drainage pattern formed during the late glacial times. The Dam and Lake have drastically disturbed the ecological balance of the Nile Valley.

44. Tifernine Dune Field, Sahara, Algeria

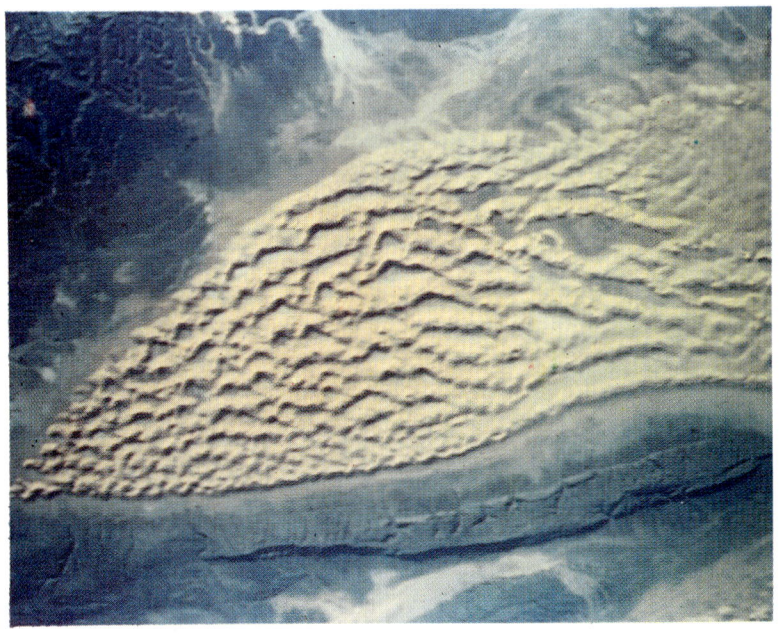

Nay, but we gave these and their fathers ease until life grew long for them. Do they not see how We visit the land, reducing it of its outlying parts? Can they be the victors? **(Qur'an 21:44)**

These dunes are a part of the most desolate parts of the Sahara. To the north of the photograph the dunes often form in long crescents with a steep, convex face, but in the south star dunes predominate; thus there is no consistent wind direction. The deeply incised gullies at lower left are drainage channels which were probably cut during the late glacial times during a period of heavy rainfall; now rainstorms are very rare.

45. Dunes of Simpson Desert, Queensland, Australia

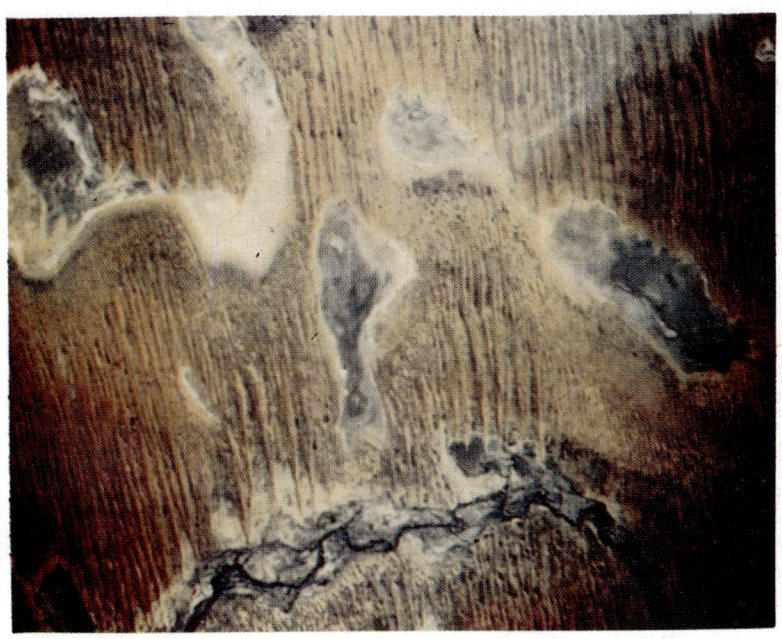

And He it is who sends the winds as a glad tiding of His mercy; and We send down pure water from the sky, so that we may give life to dead land thereby, and We give to drink there of to many beasts and men that We have created. And, indeed, many times have We repeated this unto men so that they may take it to heart; but most men refuse to be anything but ingrate. **(Qur'an 25:48-50)**

The linear streaks in the desert terrain are sand dunes, 20-30 m high, shaped by the prevailing winds. The virtually dried out lakes fill during the rainy season, and vegetation flourishes on the banks. The blue-grey areas show traces of moisture in the centers while the white are salty residues around the lakes. The Simpson Desert is so remote it was first crossed only in 1939.

46. Glaciers, Lakes, and Fault Zones, Tibet Plateau

Nay, who is He that has made the earth a fixed abode, and has placed rivers in its midst, and has set upon it firm mountains, and has placed a barrier between the two bodies of water [sweet and saltish]? Is there any divine power besides God? Nay, most of them do not know! **(Qur'an 27:61)**

The Tibet Plateau is the largest and highest elevated region in the world. In the northwest corner the ground falls away to the Tarim Basin. At top right is the snow capped mountain with valley glaciers of Muztag Ulu (7282 m). The linear valley with two lakes in the middle may be the site of strike slip fault. The blue lake in the center shows extensive terraces around its shores. The lake levels were 300 m higher during glacial times; the climate has become increasingly arid since the Ice Age ended. .

47. Coast and Andes Mountains, Chile

And We have set up firm mountains on earth, lest it sway with them, and We have appointed thereon broad paths so that they might find their way. **(Qur'an 21:31)**

The Andes is one of the longest continuous mountain ranges on Earth, and quite narrow over much of the length. Illustrated here are the Andes near Coquimbo, Chile, where the highest peaks are 6,300 m high; however, there are passes across the range whose lowest elevations are about 4,000 m. The Benioff zone both north and south of this region has well-developed volcanism. Clouds illuminated by the low sun illustrate the differences between the two sides of the Andes. The Chilean side is well-watered and fertile; the Argentine pampas in the rain shadow are very dry.

48. Glaciers, Andes Mountains, Argentina

Do they not see how We visit the earth, We reduce it from its outlying parts? For when God commands, there is none to repel His command. And He is swift in reckoning. **(Qur'an 13:41)**

The Andes mountain range near Patagonia, Argentina, is partly covered by a permanent ice cap. One glacier is seen cutting off an arm of Lake Argentina (top). Water builds up behind the glacier, and comes down in spring in a thunderous burst that is heard 40 km away. These waters and glaciers are geomorphological forces which alter the surface of the earth. As the ice and water flow down, they tear off rock and soil from valley floors and walls, cause erosion, and deposit sediment at lower elevations.

INDEX

A. Index of Proper Nouns, Arabic Key Words, and Major Subject-Areas and Topics

B. Index of Quranic Verses Quoted or Referred on a Subject or Topic: